GW01374871

BRANCH LINES AROUND SWANSEA

Vic Mitchell and Keith Smith

MP *Middleton Press*

Front cover: The Swansea & Mumbles Railway appeared to be a tramway after its electrification. Here Car 3 is attached to another as they glide close to two tank traps near Southend on 16th May 1959. (I.L.Wright)

Back cover upper: One siding at Pantyffynnon was used for stabling diesels working coal traffic. Class 37s and 08s were present on 1st September 1985. (P.Jones)

Back cover lower: Railway Clearing House map of Swansea Docks for 1913. Swansea Harbour Trust lines are not coloured.

Published January 2013

ISBN 978 1 908174 38 3

© Middleton Press, 2013

Design Deborah Esher
Typesetting Barbara Mitchell

Published by
    Middleton Press
    Easebourne Lane
    Midhurst
    West Sussex
    GU29 9AZ
Tel: 01730 813169
Fax: 01730 812601
Email: info@middletonpress.co.uk
www.middletonpress.co.uk

Printed in the United Kingdom by Henry Ling Limited, at the Dorset Press, Dorchester, DT1 1HD

CONTENTS

1. Vale of Neath Line
2. Rhondda & Swansea Bay Line
3. Garnant Branch
4. Gwaun-Cae-Gurwen Branch
5. Swansea Vale Line
6. Morriston Branch
7. Swansea District Line
8. Swansea & Mumbles Railway

INDEX

3.8	Ammanford	3.14	Glanamman	6.8	Plas Marl
3.10	Ammanford Colliery Halt	4.1	Gwaun-Cae-Gurwen	5.13	Pontardawe
2.1	Briton Ferry	5.8	Gwys	7.1	Pont Lliw
1.9	Briton Ferry Road	6.9	Landore Low Level	6.16	Swansea
5.1	Brynamman	7.2	Llangyfelach	1.10	Swansea East Dock
1.8	Cape Halt	5.19	Morriston East	5.24	Swansea Harbour Branch
5.15	Clydach-on-Tawe	6.4	Morriston West	6.13	Swansea High Street
6.6	Copper Pit Platform	1.5	Neath Abbey	5.27	Swansea North Dock
5.7	Cwmllynfell	2.5	Neath Canal Side	2.8	Swansea Riverside
6.1	Felin Fran Halt	1.1	Neath Riverside	5.24	Swansea St.Thomas
3.17	Garnant	3.1	Pantyffynon	5.21	Upper Bank
5.14	Glais	6.3	Pentrefelin (Glam) Halt	5.10	Ystalyfera

ACKNOWLEDGEMENTS

We are very grateful for the assistance received from many of those mentioned in the credits, also to B.Bennett, B.W.L.Brooksbank, A.R.Carder, G.Croughton, M.Dart, S.Davies, B.Dotson, S.C.Jenkins, N.Langridge, C.G.Maggs, J.Organ, Mr D. and Dr S.Salter, T.Walsh and in particular, our always supportive wives, Barbara Mitchell and Janet Smith.

Railway Clearing House Map for 1922. For details please see the maps for each section.
Dots show the county boundaries.

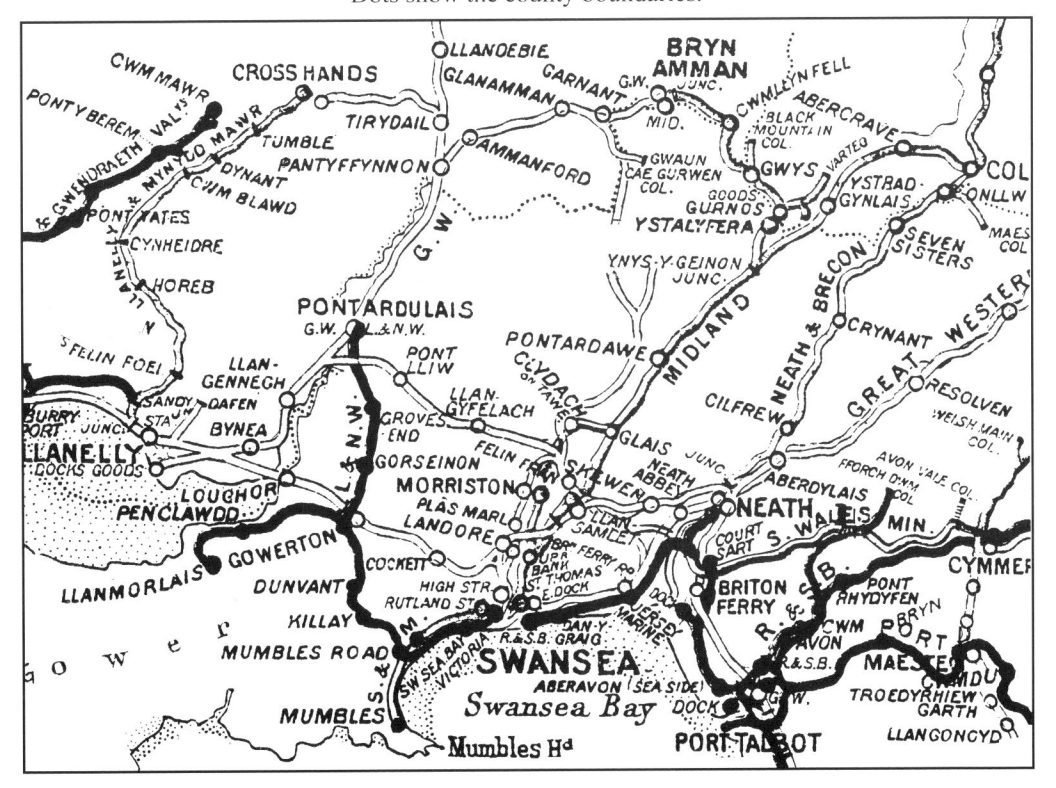

GEOGRAPHICAL SETTING

The mountainous area inland from Swansea is cut through by two major water courses, the River Loughor and the River Tawe, the city and its docks being at the mouth of the latter. Briton Ferry is close to the outflow of the River Neath. The River Amman enters the Loughor at Ammanford and trains ran close to it for over six miles.

The coal basin comes to the surface south of the Amman Valley and it is here that anthracite is still produced. This is a hard and high energy form of coal. The maps show that coal was mined extensively across the region and iron, steel, copper and chemicals were worked widely. An oil refinery was created at Llandarcy, west of Neath.

Most of the lines were built in Glamorganshire, but those in the Amman Valley were in Carmarthenshire. The headland west of Swansea is the Gower Peninsula and it has east-west bands of coal and limestone, the latter forming Mumbles Head at the west end of Swansea Bay. Swansea became a city in 1969.

The maps are to the scale of 6ins to 1 mile, unless otherwise stated and as Welsh spelling and hyphenation has varied over the years, we have generally used the form of the period. Note that Tawe has two syllables when spoken.

HISTORICAL BACKGROUND

An outline of the history of the main routes will be given here and complete dates for the local lines will follow at the start of each section.

The South Wales Railway opened from Chepstow to Swansea in 1850 and was extended to Carmarthen in 1852. It became part of the Great Western Railway in 1863 and its broad gauge track became standard in 1872.

The Vale of Neath Railway was completed between Aberdare and Neath in 1851 and mixed gauge track was available from 1863. This route was incorporated into the GWR in 1865.

Further west was the Neath & Brecon Railway, which was completed in 1864 and joined the GWR in 1922.

The Llanelly Railway & Dock Company opened its line from Llanelly to Pontardulais in 1839, extended it to Pantyffynon in 1840 and north to Duffryn (now Ammanford) in 1841. It had a branch south from Pontardulais to Swansea from 1865 and this eventually became part of the London & North Western Railway in 1891 and the London Midland & Scottish Railway in 1923. The route north and southwest of the junction was a constituent of the GWR from 1889.

Upon nationalisation in 1948, the LMSR largely formed the London Midland Region of British Railways, while the GWR became the Western Region.

Closures to passengers and freight are detailed in the captions. The section introductions include the historical background of the associated lines and also an outline of the passenger services provided on the route.

1. VALE OF NEATH LINE

The Vale of Neath Railway opened between Aberdare and Neath (Riverside) in 1851. Its broad gauge tracks became part of the GWR in 1865. The gauge was mixed from 1869 and standard from 1872. The VoNR took over the operation of the Swansea & Neath Railway (a subsidiary) early in 1863 and services began on 1st August 1863 to Swansea East Dock. The S&N thus became part of the GWR in 1865. Passenger service over the route ceased on 28th September 1936, but the Aberdare to Neath section continued to carry Pontypool Road trains until 1964. Burrows Sidings and Kings Dock were still busy with freight in 2012.

Passenger Services: The 1865 service comprised five weekday and three Sunday trains, but by 1896 there were three, weekdays only. This figure rose to eight in 1916 and by 1935 there were six trips by railmotor.

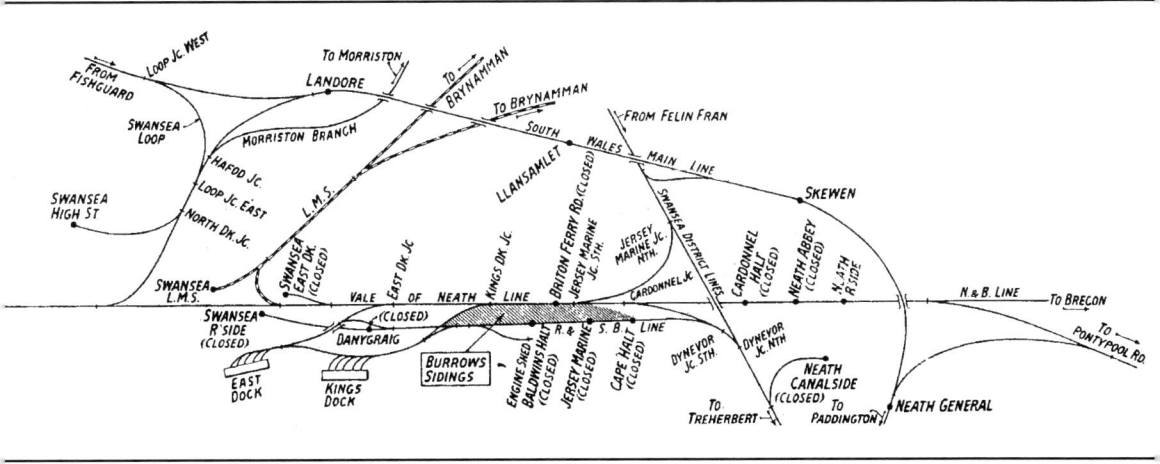

1a. 1939 diagram showing the route from Neath to Swansea from right to left.
(Railway Magazine)

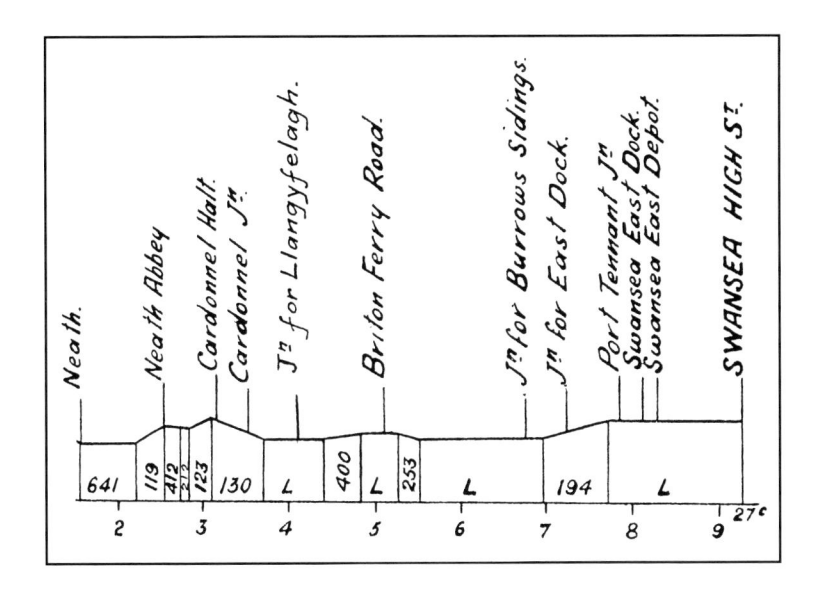

NEATH RIVERSIDE

1b. The 1935 edition has the main South Wales line from Cardiff at the lower left corner. The present station is marked **Town Sta.** The route to Swansea curves upper left. The Vale of Neath line is annotated as such (top right) and above it is the line to Brecon. In 2012, the latter still served Onllwyn for coal transport and the former did likewise for Ryans at Glyn Neath. Our first journey starts on the left bank of the river, near the road bridge, and continues southwest to the left border, close to the Tennant Canal. West of the River Neath is the Neath Canal and east of this is Neath Canal Side terminus, marked as **Sta.** This is described in caption no. 2.5. The black circles are gas holders; the gasworks has sidings from the main line.

Other albums featuring Neath are *Brecon to Neath, Cardiff to Swansea* and *Mountain Ash to Neath*.

1.1   This view north is from 10th September 1951 and shows the structures in terminal decline. All would soon be lost and only the platform on the right would be used by passengers subsequently. (H.C.Casserley)

1.2   A southward panorama from 14th July 1959 reveals that the main building was retained; it contained the booking office. The signal engineers used the yard; there is also evidence of their presence in the next two pictures. The suffix was "Low Level" in the past, but from July 1924 to September 1926 it was "Bridge Street". Thereafter, it was "Riverside". The facilities for gentlemen were under the steps. (H.C.Casserley)

1.3   The 11.25am, Saturdays Only, allowed a circular tour via Brecon, Bargoed and Cardiff, where changes were necessary. The main line passes over the bridge. The signal box was opened in 1892 and had 38 levers. It was still in use in 2012, as it controlled the junction beyond the bridge; see map 1b. (M.J.Stretton coll.)

1.4   The entrance is seen on 29th April 1961. Regular service to and from the north ceased in October 1962, but school trains called here until June 1964. The last train south had left in 1936. (R.M.Casserley)

NEATH ABBEY

1.5 This view northeast records the first public train on the Neath & Swansea Railway. Neath Abbey is on the right and the parish church is on the left. The date is 1st August 1863.
(Unknown)

1.6 Pictured on a postcard is a railmotor running east of the station. This form of transport was introduced in 1905. The ruins are behind the camera and the dominant feature is a chapel. There was a staff here of 10 in 1913, but only 3 in the 1930s.
(P.Laming coll.)

1.7 A picture from the 1950s includes part of the goods shed, behind the station building. The yard closed on 28th September 1964, but passenger traffic finished on 28th September 1936. There had been a 33-lever signal box here until 9th September 1931; It was a ground frame thereafter and until 1965.
(D.K.Jones coll.)

NEATH ABBEY

1c. The 1918 edition at 25ins to 1 mile includes Terminus Road, but this refers to the street trams of the Swansea Improvements & Tramways Company (1900-37). Inset is the 1900 map at 6ins to 1 mile to show the colliery in relation to Neath Abbey's remains, plus the sidings. The goods shed is between the station and the Picture Theatre. The Neath-Landore main line is across the top.

GREAT WESTERN RAIL
Rockfield House
Hope & Anchor (P.H.)
TRAMWAY
L.B
P.O. P.H.
Infant School
Neath 1
Swansea 7
TRAMWAY
Ebenezer Chapel (Wesleyan)
Old Limekilns
Neath Abbey (Remains of)

Bryn-clydach
Heol-draw
Old Quarry
Neath Contributory to Swansea
R.I. Ry
Parl. Boro. By
Old Quarry
Court Herbert
Neath Abbey Wks
Con.gl. Chap.
Stone
Lodge
P.H.
Sch.
Smy. Chap.
S.P.
Neath Abbey Colliery Muni. By.
S.P.
Neath Abbey (Remains of)
Spring
Stone Stone
Towing Path
Highest point to which Ordinary Tides flow

H.W.M.O.T.
Saltings
C.O.L.W.
Muni. Boro. Bdy
H.W.M.O.T.
DRY DOCK

CAPE HALT

1.8 This halt is shown incorrectly as **Cape Station** on the left page of map 2c, but appears correctly on map 2a. It was open for workmen only, but the dates are not known. To the north was Cardonnel Junction signal box, which had 33 levers and closed on 1st October 1961. North of this box was Cardonnel Halt. (Lens of Sutton coll.)

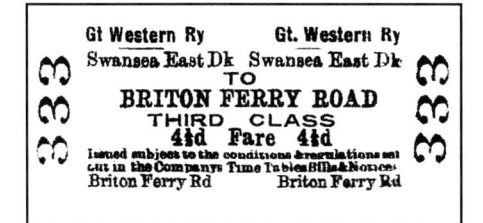

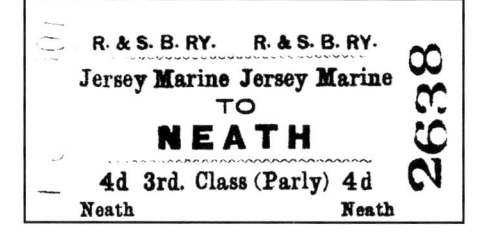

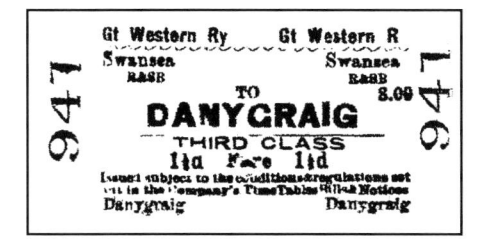

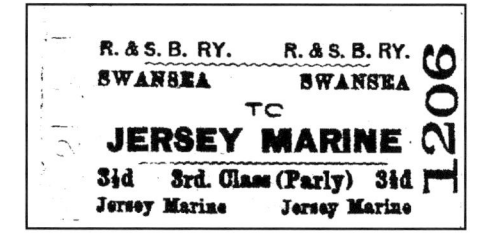

BRITON FERRY ROAD

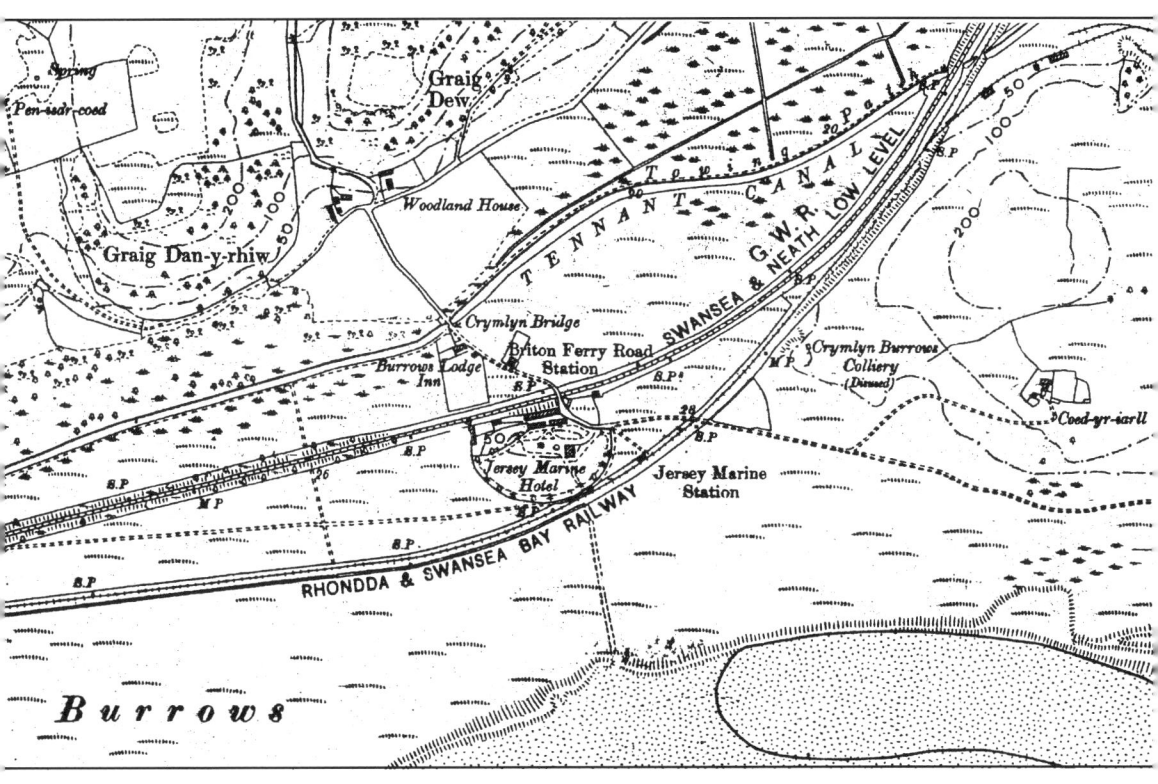

1d. The 1900 map mentions both competing railways and both stations, albeit with different names.

1.9 The tower of Jersey Marine Hotel is featured in this southward panorama. The signal box had 25 levers and was in use until 1936. North of it was Jersey Marine Junction South Box; it is on diagram 2a and mentioned in caption 2.6. (P.Laming coll.)

SWANSEA EAST DOCK

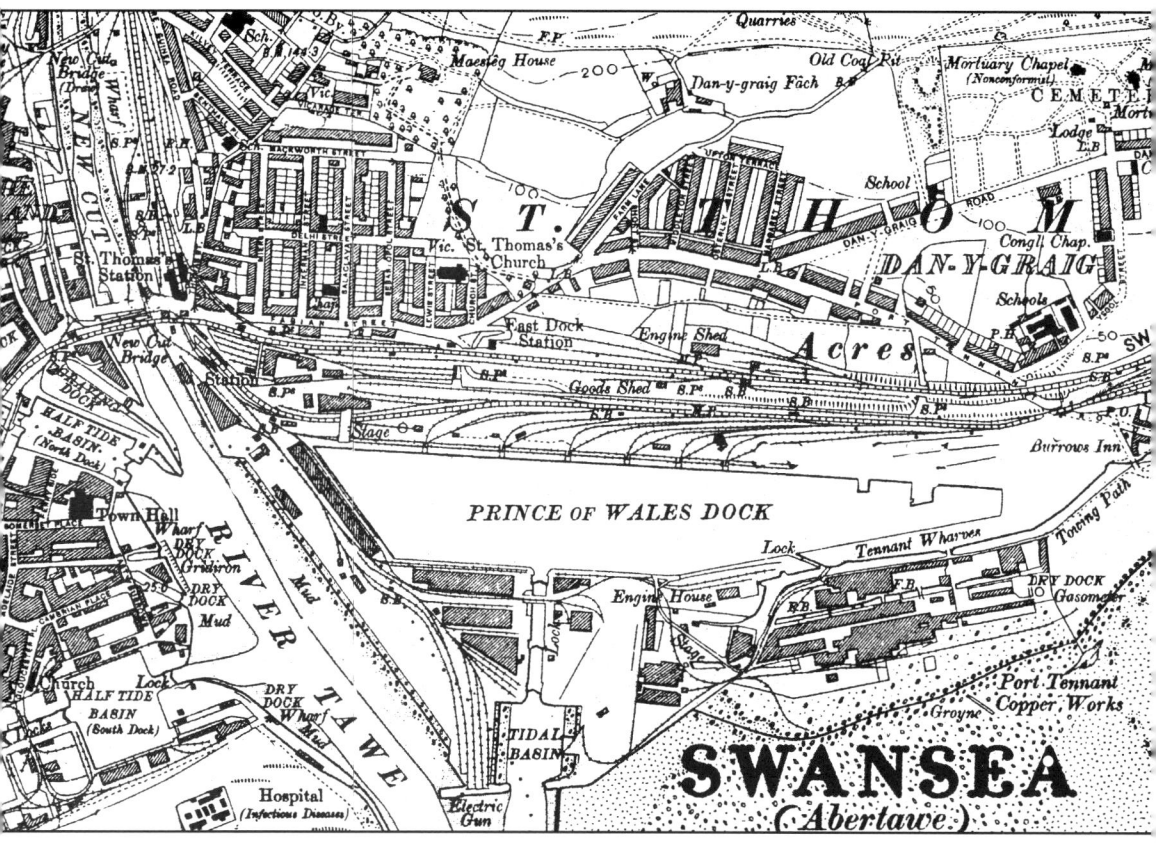

1e. Careful study of this 1900 extract shows that the canal moves from top to bottom across the right and left pages. It enters the Prince of Wales Dock, which is otherwise known as East Dock. The GWR **East Dock** terminus is above this. **Danygraig Station** is on the left page (right edge); it was open from 14th March 1895 to 7th May 1899. The GWR opened Danygraig Halt nearby on 11th September 1933, closing it on 28th September 1936. On the far left is **St. Thomas Station**, the MR terminus, and below it is the RSBR terminus. It was **South Dock** from 17th July 1924 and **Riverside** from 17th September 1926. See the diagram on the back cover.

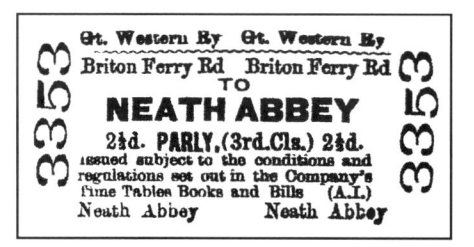

→ 1.10 East Dock terminus was in use from 1st October 1880 until 28th September 1936. The view is from about 1910 and includes the footbridge to the Prince of Wales Dock. (Lens of Sutton coll.)

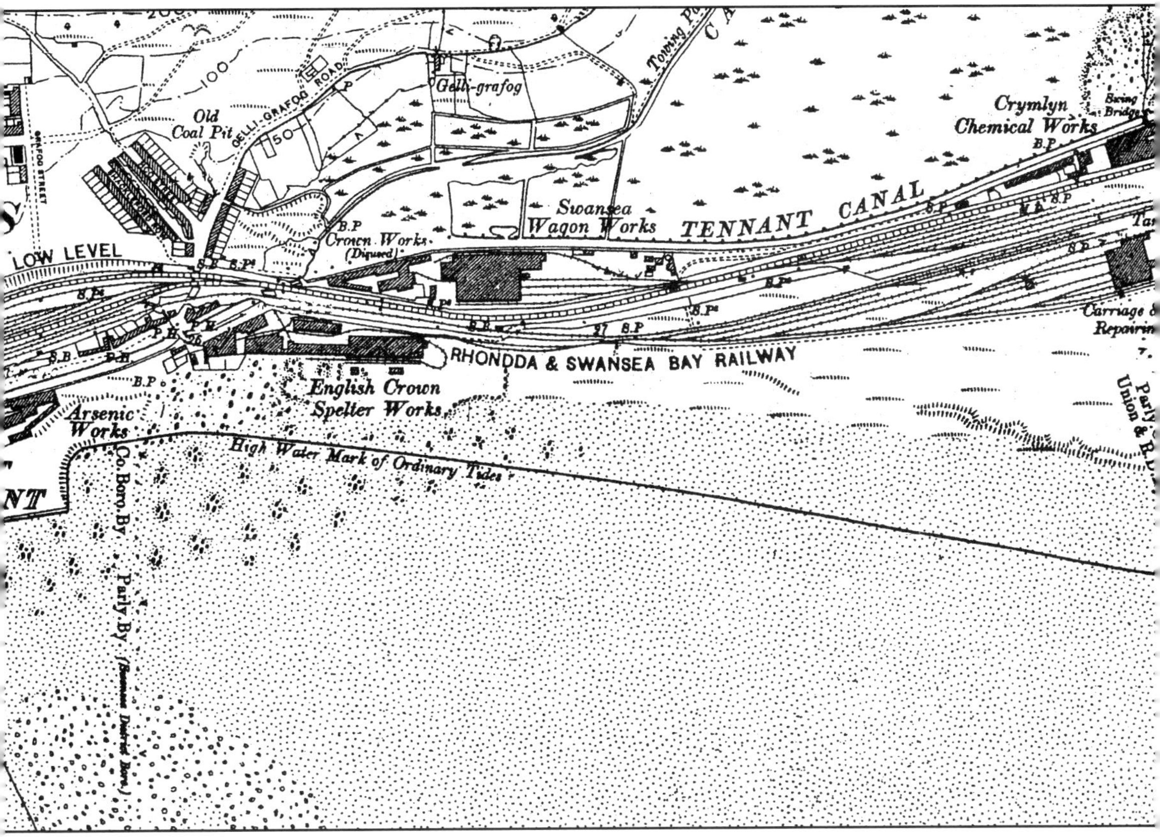
Old
Coal Pit
GELLI-GRAFOG ROAD
Gelli-grafog
Crymlyn
Chemical Works
Towing Path
Swansea
Wagon Works
TENNANT CANAL
LOW LEVEL
Crown Works
(Disused)
Carriage &
Repairing
RHONDDA & SWANSEA BAY RAILWAY
English Crown
Spelter Works
Arsenic
Works
High Water Mark of Ordinary Tides
Co. Boro. By.
Parly. By.
Parly.
Union & B.

1.11   A panorama from 10th June 1935 has standard ten-ton wagons waiting to enter the hoists when the ships arrive. (R.S.Carpenter coll.)

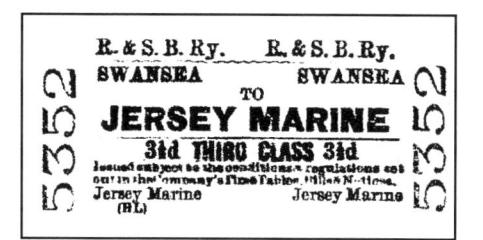

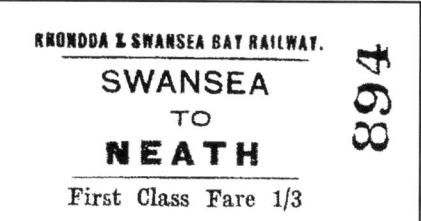

1.12 Alternative loading methods were developed, using belts. Most wagons were privately owned until 1947. (R.S.Carpenter coll.)

1.13 GWR 0-6-2T no. 6681 waits to leave East Dock on 17th August 1935. The station closed on 28th September 1936. The first terminus opened on 1st August 1863 and was called Wind Street. It disrupted coal trains and so was closed on 1st March 1873. It was over the river. (H.F.Wheeller/R.S.Carpenter coll.)

↑ 1.14 In August 1948, ex-Powlesland & Mason Peckett 0-4-0ST no. 779 of 1916 is seen approaching Swansea New Cut Swing Bridge. Initially the GWR used P&M engines to work their wagons round the docks. After the grouping in 1923 P&M's four Pecketts were taken into GWR stock. This is no. 1151. (I.L.Wright)

↑ 1.15 The platform was remarkably intact when photographed in July 1956. There was a 3-ton crane here for local traffic. (H.C.Casserley)

↓ 1.16 Map 1e includes the location of East Dock locomotive depot, which is seen on 8th September 1961. Facing us is 2-8-2T no. 7248 and nearest is 2-6-4T no. 42385. The LMR locos present were as a result of the closure of Swansea Paxton Street shed on 31st August 1959. (H.Ballantyne)

2. RHONDDA & SWANSEA BAY LINE

Before the 1922 amalgamations, the Rhondda & Swansea Bay Railway paralleled lines of the Great Western Railway from Briton Ferry to Court Sart, and again from Dynevor Junction to its terminus at the Riverside station, Swansea. One of the most beneficial features of the 1921 Railways Act was the ease with which it enabled uneconomical parallel lines to be turned to good account either by the separation of different classes of traffic or by the abandonment of redundant works. A scheme was devised for diverting the passenger traffic of the R&SB line onto the Great Western metals, where they provided a suitable alternative route, using part of the former exclusively for mineral traffic from the two systems and in addition abandoning certain sections and stations of the R&SB.

Under this scheme the marshalling sidings at Burrows, between Briton Ferry Road and the docks at Swansea, were enlarged and remodelled, and these, together with the old R&SB double track between these points, were handed over for the exclusive use of the Docks Department for its traffic. The abandonment of the Swansea end of the line and the diversion of the passenger trains further contributed to the more efficient working made possible by the improvements. R&SB passenger traffic was diverted by the main line from Briton Ferry to Swansea High Street. Down coal traffic was diverted at Dynevor North junction, which was single thence to Jersey Marine Junction South, at which point a new double line junction was laid in. At this junction, all goods and mineral trains, both of GWR and R&SB origin, were diverted on to the former R&SB line, with the exception of trains already sorted for shipment which went to the former reception sidings. The extensive Burrows sidings were enlarged to accommodate 1782 extra wagons. The dates of the alterations to the various passenger train facilities in this district are as follows: the R&SB service from Jersey Marine to Swansea Riverside was withdrawn on 11th September 1933, the R&SB service from Court Sart to Neath Canalside was withdrawn on 17th September 1935, and these two stations closed. After 1935, trains from the Rhondda to Swansea High Street, ran via Neath General.

Passenger Services:
The table gives down train freqency in selected years.

	Weekdays	Sundays
1896	7	2
1916	6	2
1932	8	0

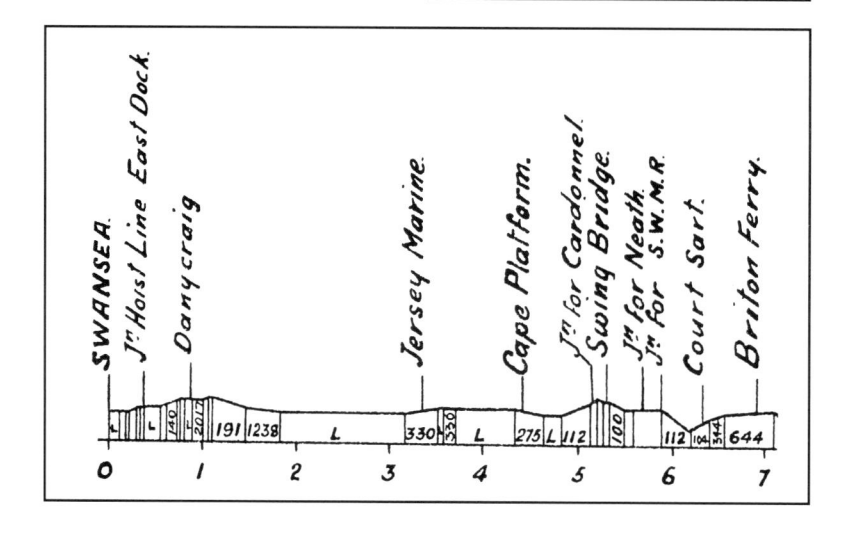

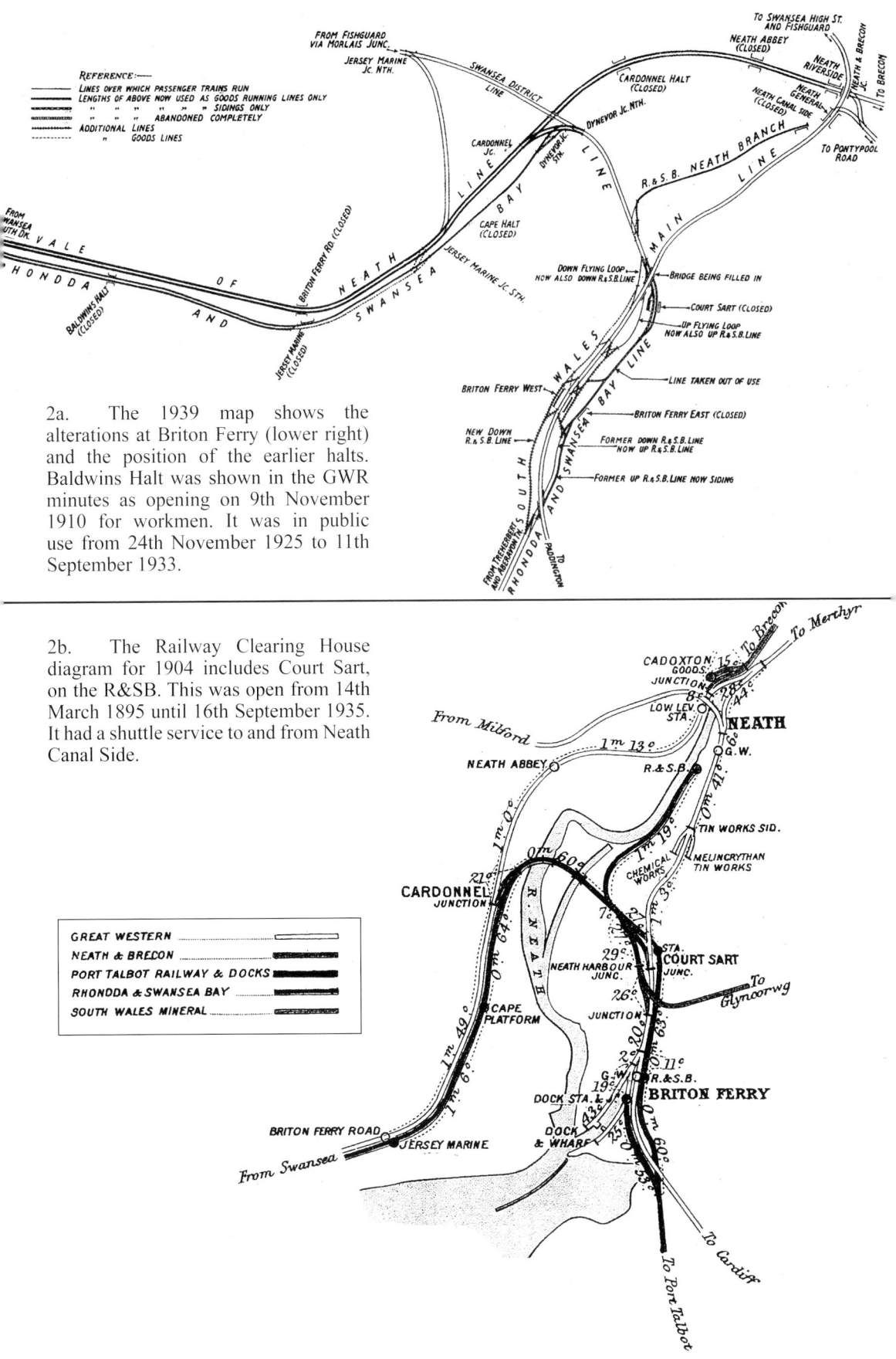

2a. The 1939 map shows the alterations at Briton Ferry (lower right) and the position of the earlier halts. Baldwins Halt was shown in the GWR minutes as opening on 9th November 1910 for workmen. It was in public use from 24th November 1925 to 11th September 1933.

2b. The Railway Clearing House diagram for 1904 includes Court Sart, on the R&SB. This was open from 14th March 1895 until 16th September 1935. It had a shuttle service to and from Neath Canal Side.

BRITON FERRY

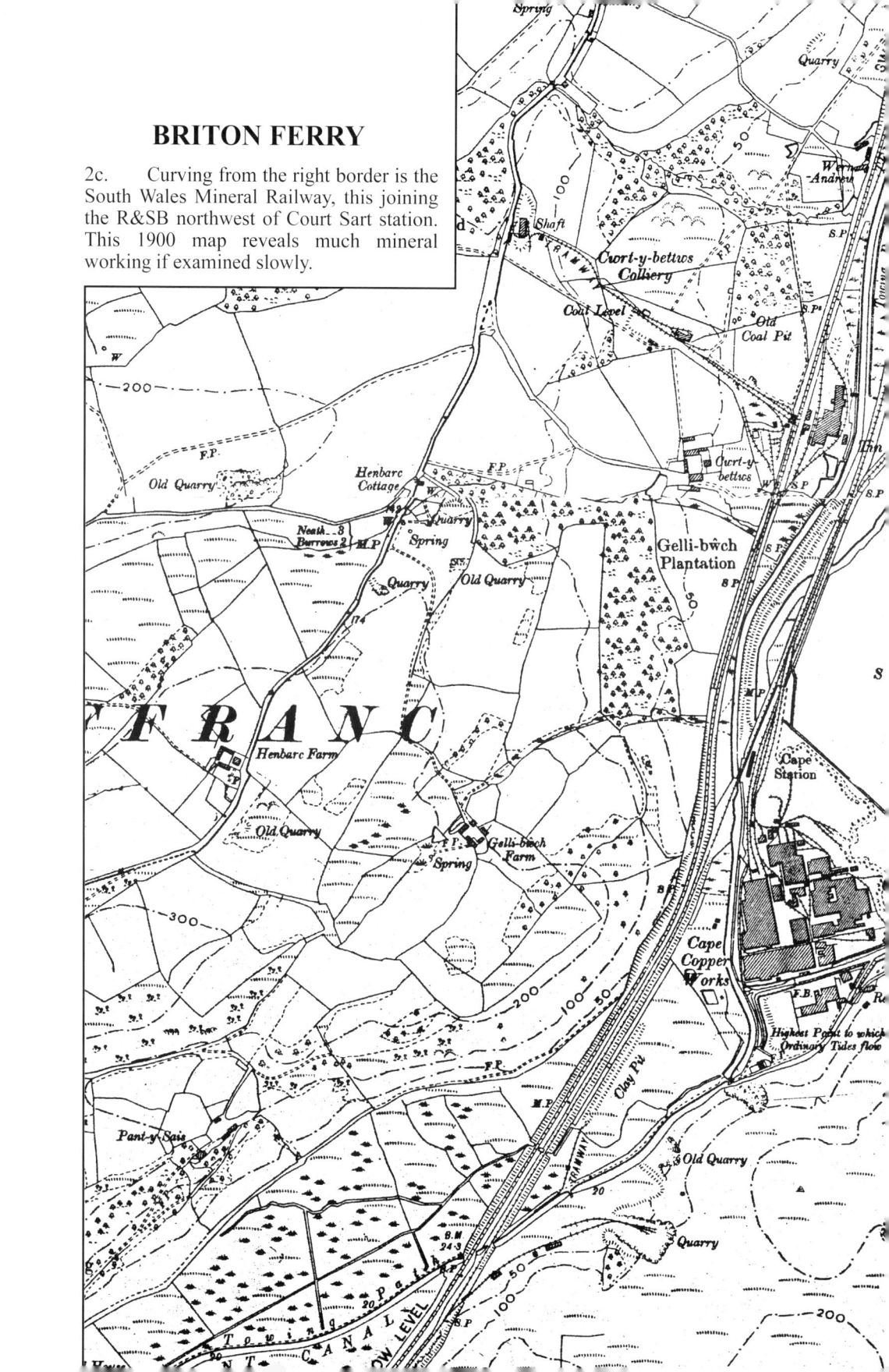

2c. Curving from the right border is the South Wales Mineral Railway, this joining the R&SB northwest of Court Sart station. This 1900 map reveals much mineral working if examined slowly.

RHONDDA & SWANSEA BAY RY.
RHONDDA & SWANSEA BAY
NEATH BRANCH
Clay Pit
RIVER NEATH
(Afon Nedd)
NEATH ABBEY WHARF
High Water Mark of Ordinary Tides
TRAMWAY
H. W. M. O. T.
Mud
Sand & Mud
U. D. B.
Post
U. D. B.
Pont y Lady
NEATH CANAL
Parly. & Munl. Boro. By.
Richmond Terrace
Maes-gwyn
Towing Path
G. W. R.
Locomotive & Carriage Repairing Works
Eastbourne Terrace
Court-Sart Farm
PANT-YR-HEOL
Hotel
Church
Court Sart Station
SOUTH WALES MINERAL RAILWAY
G. W. R.
Crossing
Saltings
Old Quarry
Hospital
BASIN
NEATH CANAL
Towing path
Old Quarry
Zoar Chapel
Inn
St. John the Baptist's Church
Giant's Grave
Pier
Giant's Arms (P.H.)
The Elms
Neath 2
Aberavon 4
RHONDDA & SWANSEA BAY RAILWAY
Old Quarry
Shelone
BRITON FERRY
(Llansawel)
Earls Wood
Shelone Wood
Shelone Road
Navvies' Well
Earlswood Tin Plate Wks.
JERSEY CANAL
Sand & Mud
Earlswood House
Vernon House
Gas Works
Church
Chap
Vernon Arms Hotel
Briton Ferry (Site of)
Earlswood Colliery (Disused)
Stage Ferry
Old Lookout
Warren Hill
TRAMWAY
Briton Ferry Iron Works
Rehoboth Chapel
School

2.1   The station on the main line opened on 2nd September 1850 and the GWR buildings were recorded on a postcard, looking north. Its location is lower right on maps 2c and 2d. It was replaced by one with four platforms, further north, on 16th September 1935. (P.Laming coll.)

2.2   A southward panorama from June 1963 shows the four gently curving platforms, with part of the massive Albion Steelworks in the distance. The station was closed on 2nd November 1964 and soon little evidence remained. (P.J.Garland/R.S.Carpenter)

BRITON FERRY
(Llansawel)

2d. The main line station is fairly obvious on this 1918 extract at 25ins to 1 mile. Less so is the single platform of the R&SB, which is between the back yards of the dwellings in Railway Terrace and Lowther Street. **East** and **West** were added to their names on 1st July 1924. Both were closed on 16th September 1935, when a larger one opened to the north of them. **Stn.** marks the entrance passage to the single platform. There was a staff of 41 in 1913, 64 in 1923 and 58 in the early 1930s.

Other views can be found in our *Cardiff to Swansea* album.

2.3   No. 37233 passes the site with oil tanks on 20th September 1979. The nearby Llandarcy Oil Refinery received much imported crude oil by rail from Swansea Docks and refined products ran in this direction. (T.Heavyside)

2.4   A fourth station came into use on 1st June 1994, further north, and is seen on 23rd August 2008, looking north. On the right is the track from Dynevor Junction, on the Swansea District Line. The connection is known as "Up Flying Loop". Down trains for that line diverge at Court Sart Junction, further north. (N.Sprinks)

NEATH CANAL SIDE

2.5   The branch is seen to diverge from the R&SB route near the tops of maps 2a, 2b and 2c. The station was open to passengers from 14th March 1895 until 16th September 1935, although the branch was in use from 1894 until 6th September 1965. It is seen from the buffers on 14th July 1956, as ex-GWR 0-6-0PT no. 7720 was about to reverse with a railtour. The terminus appears on map 1b and was named "Canal Bridge" from 1st July 1924 until 17th September 1926. (H.C.Casserley)

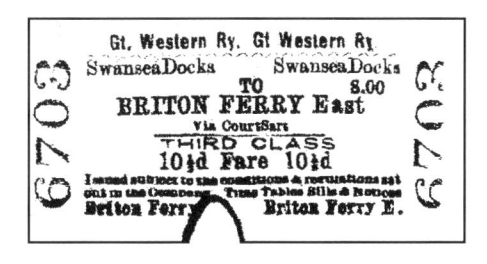

NORTH OF JERSEY MARINE

2.6   Jersey Marine Junction South was recorded from the railtour seen in 2.5, as no. 8483 passes. The location is shown on map 2a. The signal box had 54 levers and closed on 27th February 1973. The 17-lever box at Jersey Marine closed in 1933. The station was open from 14th March 1895 until 11th September 1933. (H.C.Casserley)

2.7   Danygraig Depot is shown on the extreme right of the right page of map 1e, but it was not for C&W solely. The west elevation is seen in 1958, when it was coded 87C. It had an allocation of 47 tank locomotives in 1947 and closed to steam in March 1964. The southern three sidings served the C&W section and the raised roof was over the lifting shop. (D.K.Jones coll.)

SWANSEA RIVERSIDE

2.8   The approach to the terminus was recorded on 8th September 1951, together with the pit used by locomotive crews for inside motion maintenance before departure. The station was in use from 14th March 1895 until 11th September 1933. "South Docks" was the suffix from 1st July 1924 and "Riverside" was used from 17th September 1926 until closure. (H.C.Casserley)

2.9   A view towards the buffers on the same day includes the bridge carrying the tracks to New Cut Bridge, which is shown on the left of the left page of map 1e. The adjacent goods yard was closed in August 1922. There were 20 employees here in 1930. (H.C.Casserley)

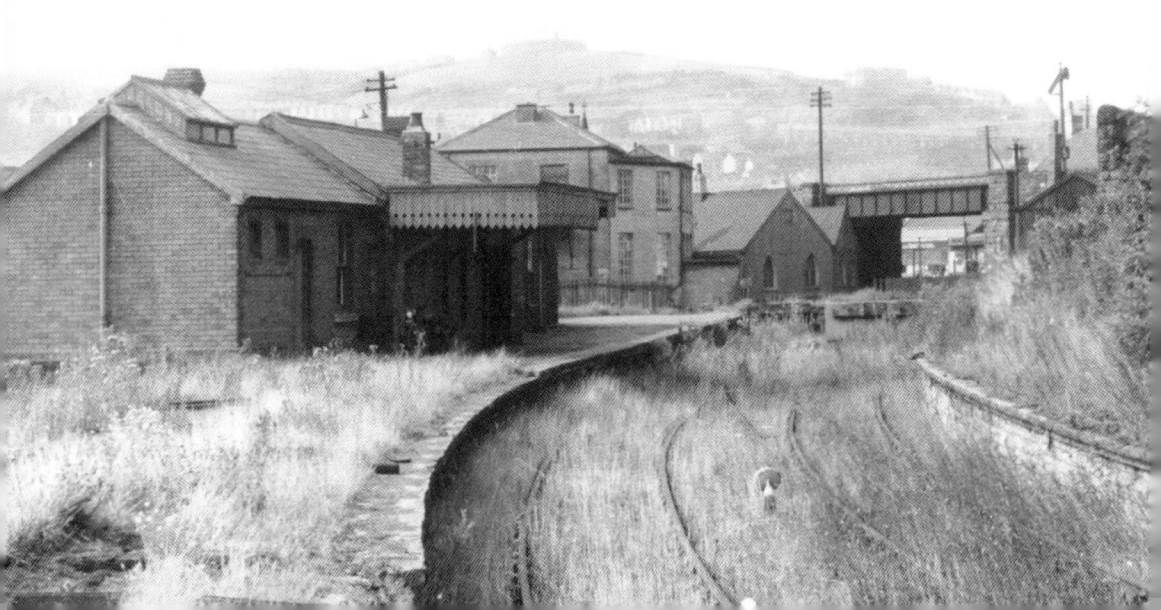

SWANSEA KINGS DOCK

2.10 No. 37159 was captured shunting wagons at the east end of the dock on 23rd August 1978. (H.Ballantyne)

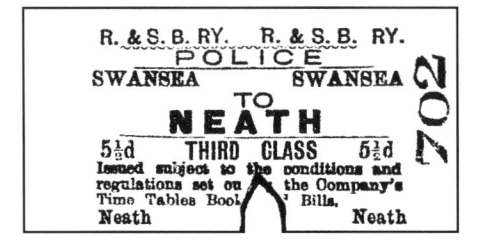

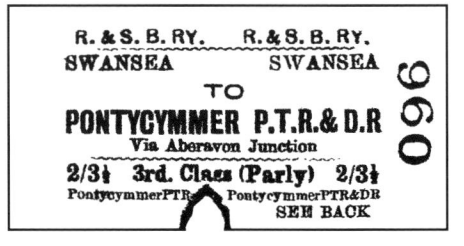

3. GARNANT BRANCH

The anthracite coalfield in the Amman Valley was first connected with the railway system when the Llanelly Railway & Dock Company opened its line from Pontardulais to Garnant on 10th April, 1840. This was extended to Gwaun-Cae-Gurwen (or GCG, as it is usually called) on 6th May 1841; in June 1842 Garnant became a junction when the line was opened from there to Brynamman.

A passenger service began on 1st May 1850, with one intermediate station on the branch at Cross Inn; this was called Ammanford from 1883 until passenger services ceased on the route on 18th August 1958. This name was used for the first station north of Pantyffynon from 1960 and both were still in use by Central Wales Line trains in 2012.

The LR&DC became part of the GWR in 1889. The Garnant to Brynamman section carried passengers from 20th March 1865 until 1958. The terminus is detailed in Section 5.

Passenger Services: Branch train frequency.

	Weekdays	Sundays
1869	2	0
1910	7	2
1935	7	0
1957	4	0

3a. This diagram shows the ownerships in 1920 and has the Swansea District Line lower left. The three stations on it opened in 1922-23; Pontrefelin Halt is not shown. The triangle at Hendy Junction (left) enabled coal from the Amman Valley to reach the docks without reversal.

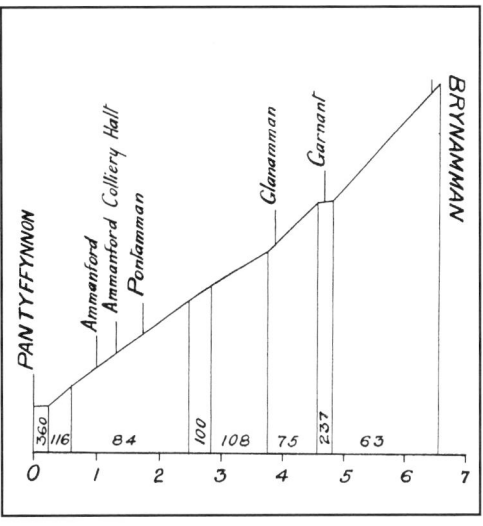

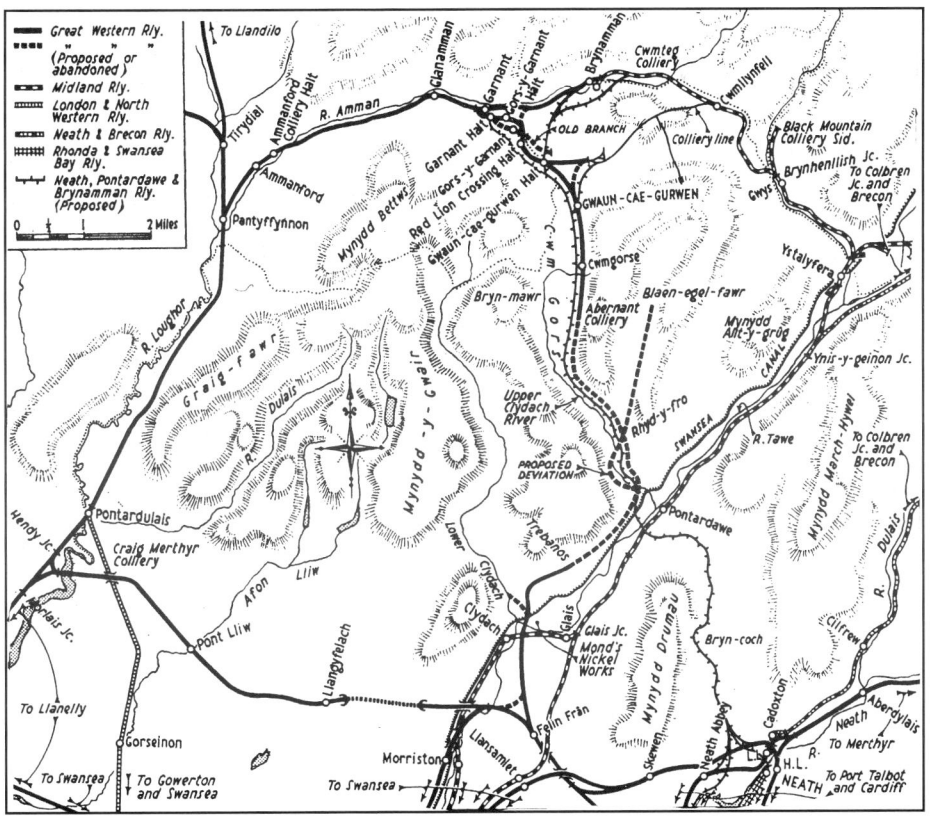

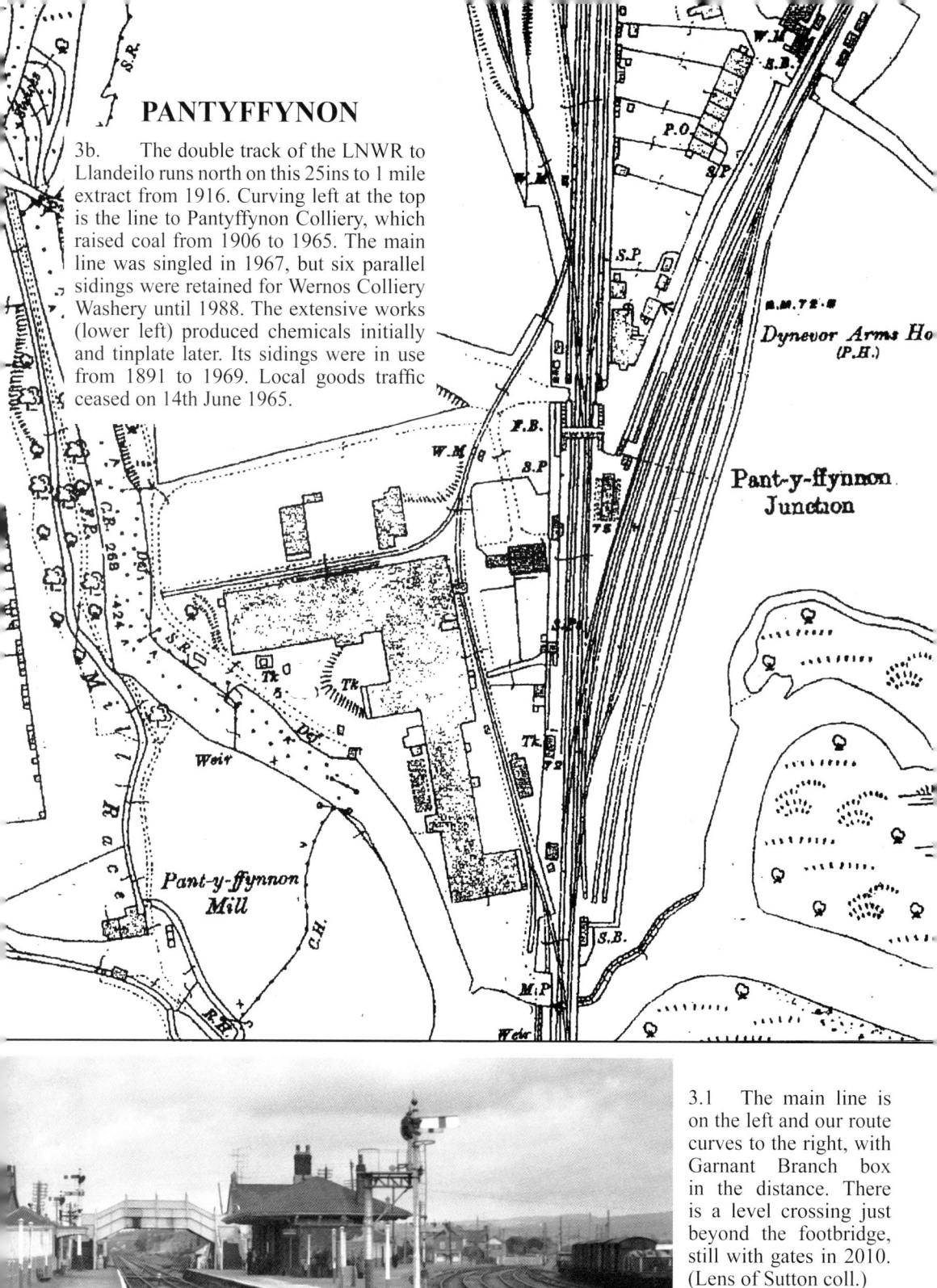

PANTYFFYNON

3b. The double track of the LNWR to Llandeilo runs north on this 25ins to 1 mile extract from 1916. Curving left at the top is the line to Pantyffynon Colliery, which raised coal from 1906 to 1965. The main line was singled in 1967, but six parallel sidings were retained for Wernos Colliery Washery until 1988. The extensive works (lower left) produced chemicals initially and tinplate later. Its sidings were in use from 1891 to 1969. Local goods traffic ceased on 14th June 1965.

3.1 The main line is on the left and our route curves to the right, with Garnant Branch box in the distance. There is a level crossing just beyond the footbridge, still with gates in 2010. (Lens of Sutton coll.)

3.2 This is the vista presented to a passenger leaving a down train. The horse waits to use the level crossing and on the right is the Garnant branch.
(Lens of Sutton coll.)

3.3 The Brunel style Chalet building is seen from the branch platform, along with South Box. It had 25 levers and became Pantyfynnon Junction Box on 16th January 1964. It was still in use in 2012, controlling 79 miles of the Central Wales Line.
(Lens of Sutton coll.)

3.4 It is July 1958 and we gain a glimpse of the engine shed, which was in use from March 1931 to August 1964. The allocation was 15 tank engines at the end of 1947. The tank on the left has the coal stage under it, this being a widely used GWR design. The code was Sub to 87F, but Sub to LY in GWR days. The location was on the west side of the branch, which is to the right of the engine. To the right of it is New Yard, the five sidings of which were in use in 1936 to 1991.
(G.Adams/
M.J.Stretton coll.)

3.5 The level crossing is top right on map 3b and was photographed on 14th September 1973, as nos 6606 and 6839 were running south. Garnant Branch signal box had been on the left from 1892 to 10th June 1968, its 25-lever frame controlling access to the locomotive depot, which had been in the background. There was a private siding across its site from 1967 to 1982. (D.H.Mitchell)

3.6 We move back to the former South Box on 28th April 2009 to watch no. 66083 about to run onto the branch at 11.59. (H.Williams)

The station is illustrated in the *Llandeilo to Swansea* album from Middleton Press.

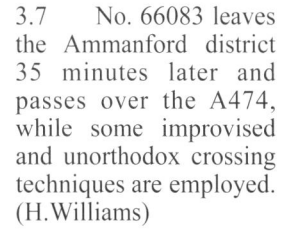

3.7 No. 66083 leaves the Ammanford district 35 minutes later and passes over the A474, while some improvised and unorthodox crossing techniques are employed. (H.Williams)

AMMANFORD

3.8 The tiny station was recorded soon after closure. The population had reached 6200 three years later and the name was transferred to the station on the CWL. Employees numbered 17 for much of the 1930s. (R.S.Carpenter coll.)

Ammanford	1903	1913	1923	1933
Passenger tickets issued	43,474	94147	46234	17331
Season tickets issued`	*	*	152	1
Parcels forwarded	10515	24244	28271	36523
General goods forwarded (tons)	869	1518	1069	843
Coal and coke received (tons)	656	482	246	2384
Other minerals received (tons)	4899	5721	1622	2484
General goods received (tons)	7061	10231	7883	19774
Coal and Coke handled	8915	19956	12949	192173
Trucks of livestock handled	-	-	1	39

3.9 Seen on 1st September 1985 is no. 37142 working on the bidirectional loop. The box had 32 levers and closed on 27th October 1990; full lifting barriers were soon installed. There had been three private sidings and a goods yard beyond the gates. Goods continued until 1964 and coal until 1988. (P.Jones)

AMMANFORD

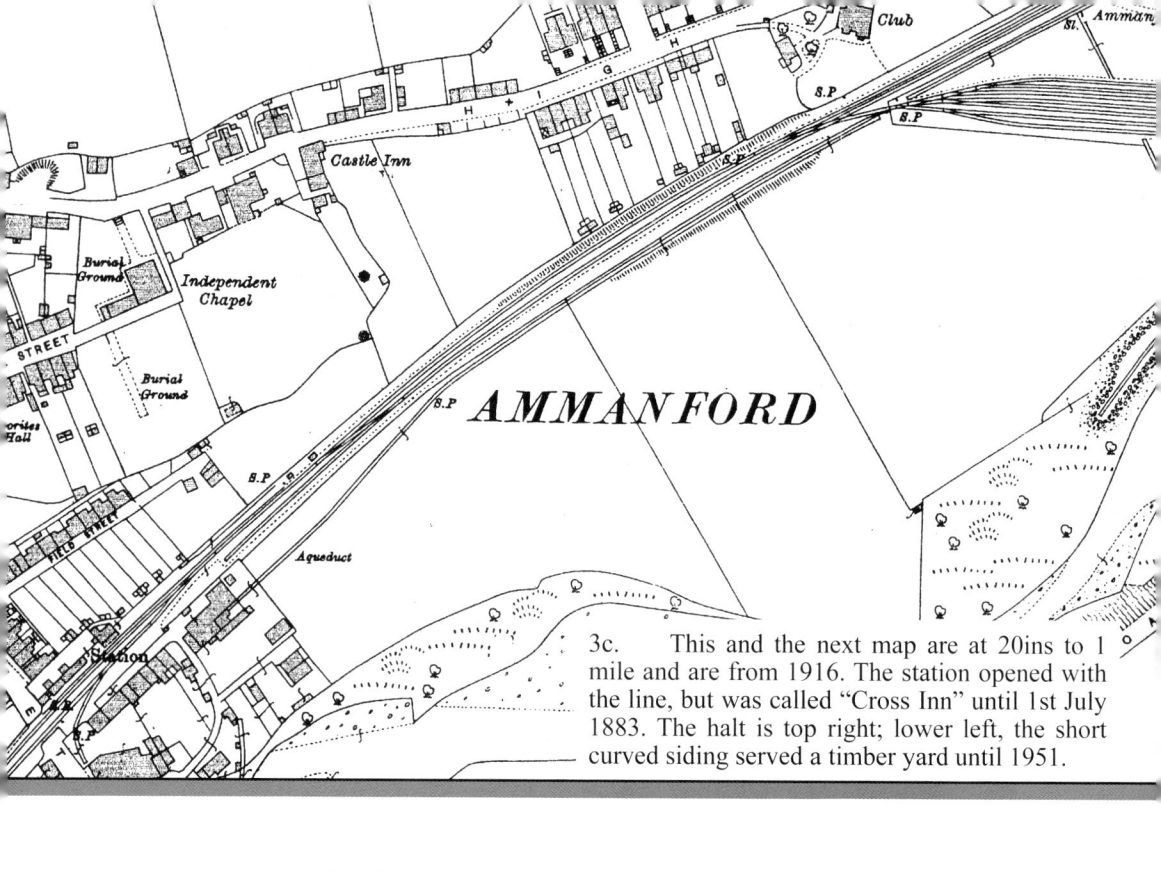

3c.   This and the next map are at 20ins to 1 mile and are from 1916. The station opened with the line, but was called "Cross Inn" until 1st July 1883. The halt is top right; lower left, the short curved siding served a timber yard until 1951.

AMMANFORD COLLIERY HALT

3d.   This extract continues from the previous one and includes the triangle which allowed coal traffic to flow in two directions.

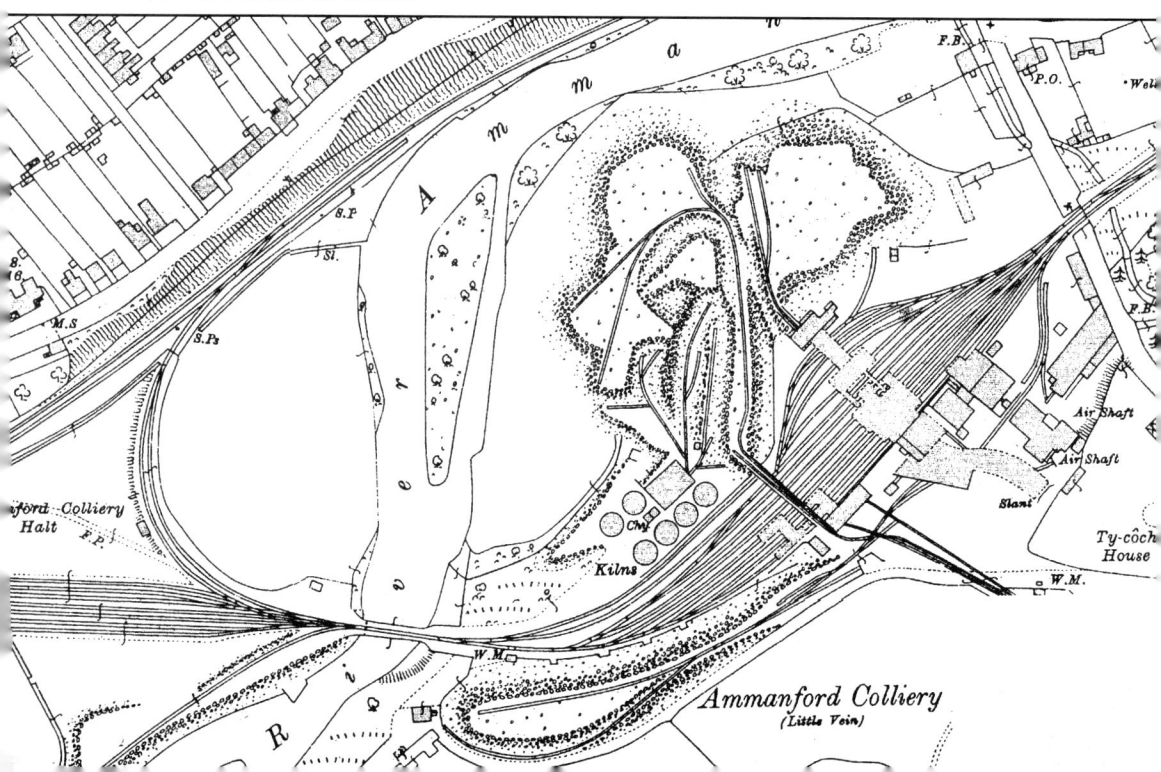

3.10 A 1912 view reveals the extent of the loading facilities. This was a slant mine, where chains hauled loaded wagons up a 1 in 4 incline. Opencast working became widespread in the area of this album during World War II and after. (GWR)

3.11 The halt was in use from 1st May 1905 until 18th August 1958 and is seen in 1964. Locals have regularly used the route as a footpath and subsequent periods of disuse have aggravated the problem. (Stations UK)

3.12 Turning round, we see the 25-lever box, which was functional until 23rd July 1964. The colliery lines were in use from 1892 to 1975. New sidings were laid on almost the same site for Bettws New Mine in 1978 and they lasted until 1984. (Stations UK)

EAST OF AMMANFORD

3.13 In less than ½ mile, the branch crosses the River Amman, but only one track was present here and through the 330yd long Pontamman Tunnel. No. 37297 runs west with coal on 19th September 1979. (T.Heavyside)

3e.   Two active collieries and several defunct ones are included on this 1948 extract. Gellyceidrim Colliery (right) had rail connection from 1890 until 1955.

3.14   Local industry is evident in this pre-1914 photograph with loaded anthracite on the right and a tinplate works in the background. It had sidings from 1897 to 1952. The GWR employed ten between 1913 and 1932 at this station. (GWR)

Glanamman	1903	1913	1923	1933
Passenger tickets issued	28585	73877	29260	9051
Season tickets issued	*	*	252	70
Parcels forwarded	2611	7850	5069	6114
General goods forwarded (tons)	-	18108	14379	183
Coal and coke received (tons)	-	12137	6872	-
Other minerals received (tons)	-	21037	15207	167
General goods received (tons)	-	13917	7841	4110
Coal and Coke handled	-	4785	7504	91377
Trucks of livestock handled	-	109	138	60

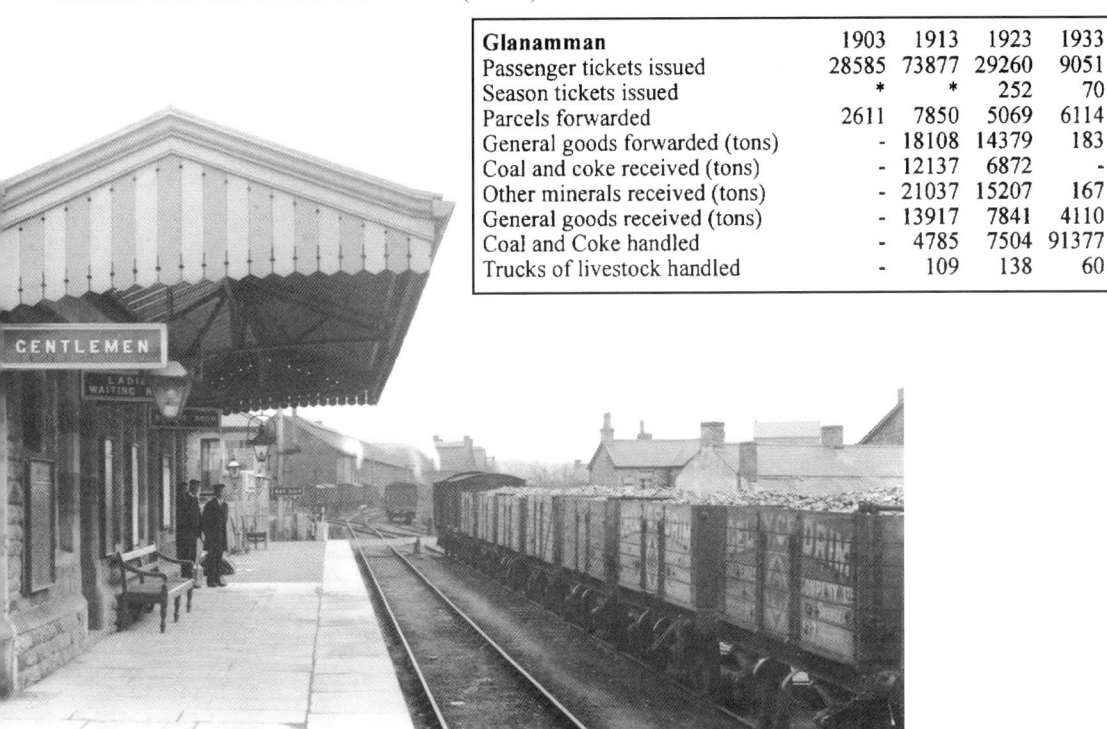

3.15   Working up the valley just prior to closure was 0-6-0PT no. 7718. The station opened in about May 1851 and was called "Cross Keys" until 1st December 1884. The signal box had 33 levers and lasted until 21st July 1990. It only controlled the crossing from 1964, this having barriers from 1976. (C.L.Caddy)

3.16   We are looking in the other direction in 1964 as dismantling proceeds. The loop had been taken out of use that year. The next station east was Gellyceidrim; it was open from 1852 to 1861 only. (Stations UK)

GARNANT

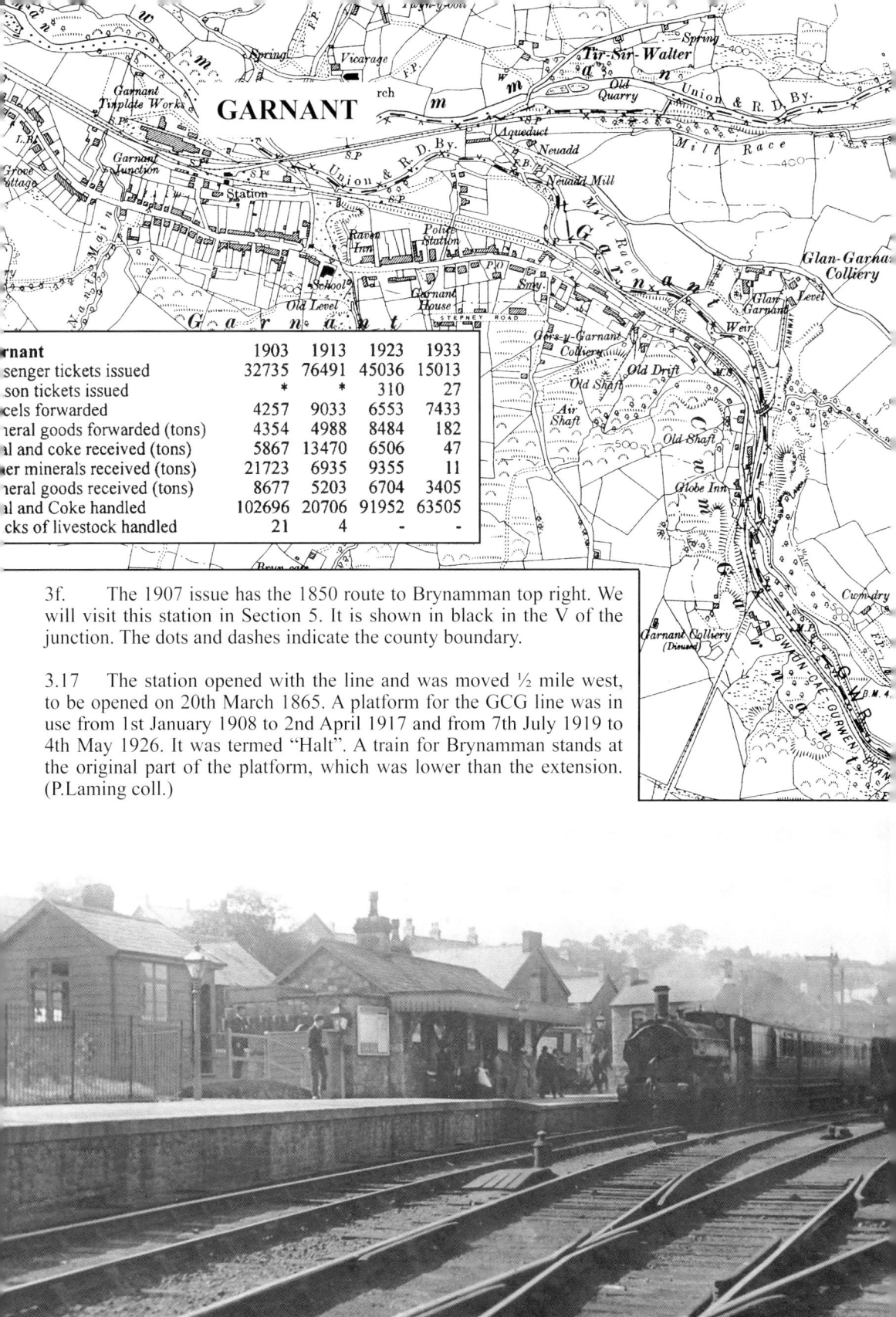

	1903	1913	1923	1933
...senger tickets issued	32735	76491	45036	15013
...son tickets issued	*	*	310	27
...cels forwarded	4257	9033	6553	7433
...neral goods forwarded (tons)	4354	4988	8484	182
...al and coke received (tons)	5867	13470	6506	47
...er minerals received (tons)	21723	6935	9355	11
...neral goods received (tons)	8677	5203	6704	3405
...al and Coke handled	102696	20706	91952	63505
...cks of livestock handled	21	4	-	-

3f. The 1907 issue has the 1850 route to Brynamman top right. We will visit this station in Section 5. It is shown in black in the V of the junction. The dots and dashes indicate the county boundary.

3.17 The station opened with the line and was moved ½ mile west, to be opened on 20th March 1865. A platform for the GCG line was in use from 1st January 1908 to 2nd April 1917 and from 7th July 1919 to 4th May 1926. It was termed "Halt". A train for Brynamman stands at the original part of the platform, which was lower than the extension. (P.Laming coll.)

3.18   Female fashion seldom features in our albums; maybe this panorama was for the benefit of students of oil lighting. The staff numbered 28 in 1903, dropping to 15 by 1932. (P.Laming coll.)

3.19   A 1964 photograph allows us to look east after the canopy had been removed. The line to Brynamman is on the left and the GCG one is on the right. The box had 46 levers and was working until 23rd July 1964. (Stations UK)

4. GWAUN-CAE-GURWEN BRANCH

The extension from Garnant was opened for coal traffic by the LR&DC in 1841. The route was realigned by the GWR, the old line becoming known as the Cawdor Branch. The new branch opened for freight on 4th November 1907. At Gwaun-Cae-Gurwen there was a signal box controlling the level crossing and the entrance to a group of sidings. From there lines continued to the east and south to serve three collieries, and made connection with a colliery line which joined the former Midland branch just west of Cwmllynfell station, at a signalbox which was also called Gwaun-Cae-Gurwen.

On 1st January 1908, the GWR inaugurated a passenger service from Garnant to Gwaun-Cae-Gurwen by a steam railcar. Halts were opened at Gors-y-Garnant, Red Lion Crossing and the terminus; the latter was just west of the level crossing. The service was withdrawn on 4th May 1926.

In 1911, the GWR obtained powers for a railway, about ten miles long, from triangular junctions at Gwaun-Cae-Gurwen southwards to Felin Fran on the Swansea District line, then under construction, but succeeded in carrying out only part of the scheme because of interruption by World War I. The northern section of the main line, from GCG to Duke Colliery, 2½ miles, was opened to goods traffic on 3rd August 1923. This section was revived in 1961 by the new anthracite colliery of Abernant, under construction.

Though single it was constructed for double tracks and had two substantial "ghost" stations, Gwaun-Cae-Gurwen, some half-mile from the earlier halt, and Cwmgorse. Neither ever saw passenger traffic, but the former provided goods and parcels facilities until 7th May 1965.

Passenger Services:
Eight return trips by a railmotor on most weekdays ran during the period stated.

GWAUN-CAE-GURWEN

4.1 This viaduct was on the second route and was 98yds long. The earlier one was shorter and was downstream of this. (P.Laming coll.)

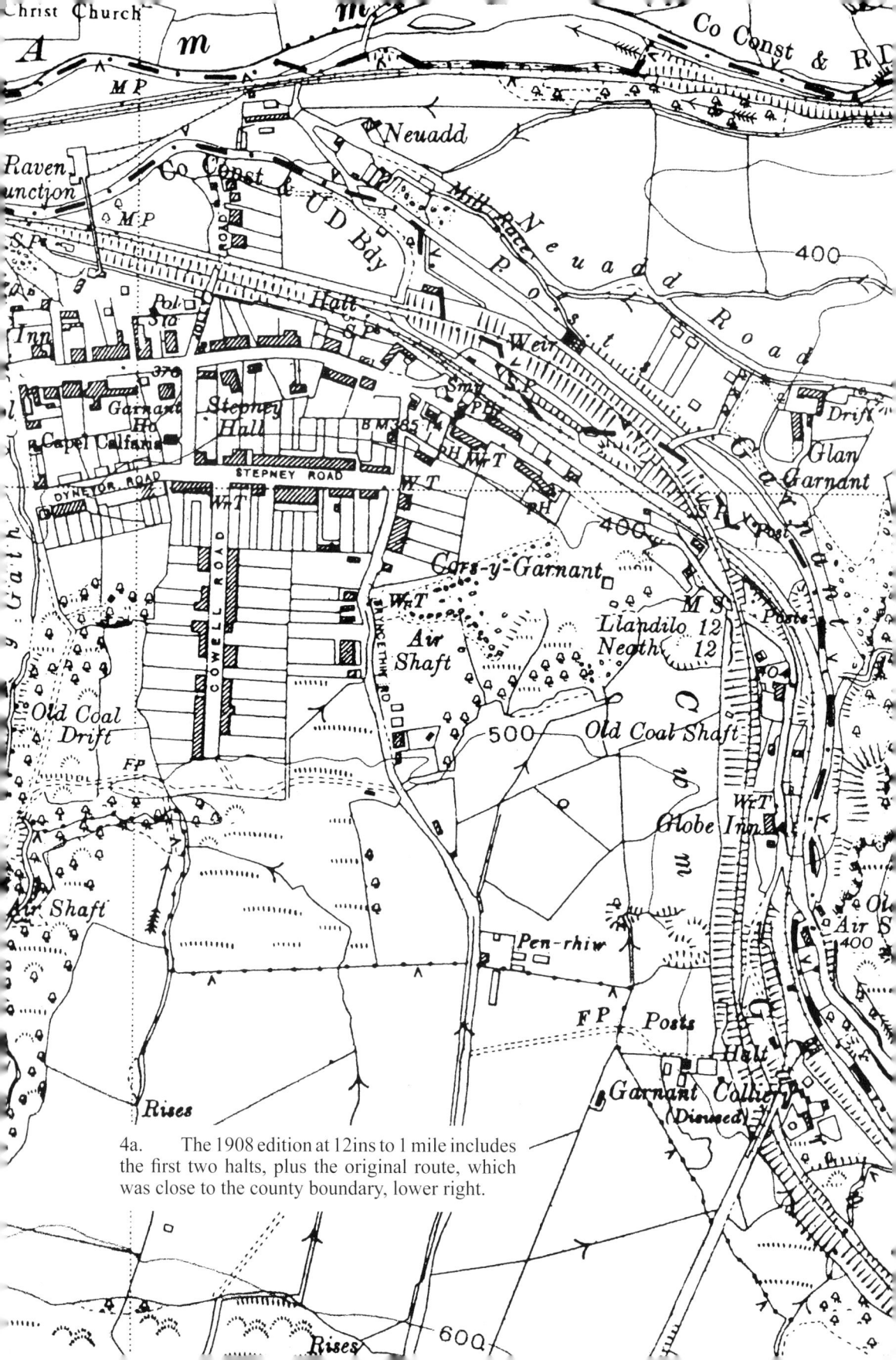

4a. The 1908 edition at 12ins to 1 mile includes the first two halts, plus the original route, which was close to the county boundary, lower right.

4.2 The signal box was open from 1st January 1908 until 4th May 1926 and had 17 levers. The station dates were the same, but it was also closed in 1917-19, due to wartime economy measures. Employees numbered eleven in 1913 and six in 1929. Coal tonnages forwarded in those years were 54,000 and 56,000. (P.Laming coll.)

4.3 The box met its end in 1973 when hit by a derailed coal train. It had served as a ground frame from July 1964. Seen on 2nd July 1955 is ex-LMS class 3F no. 47480 with an SLS tour train. (T.J.Edgington)

4.4   The branch was never officially closed, but has had lengthy periods of disuse. Service was resumed on 16th January 2009 after no trains ran for about ten years. Anthracite was conveyed from the opencast site here to the washery at Onllwyn. No. 66076 was recorded on that day. (P.Lee)

SOUTH OF GWAUN-CAE-GURWEN

4.5   This is Cwmgorse, one of the two stations built but never opened. The General Strike was given as the reason. (A.Muckley)

4.6 Abernant Colliery sidings were recorded on 1st September 1985 as Type 3 diesels nos 37237 and 37220 stood by the former Inwards Empties sidings. The traffic began on 24th January 1966. (P.Jones)

4.7 Two class 37s were working on 11th May 1989, but coal was not raised after 1988. There were 12 parallel sidings and they were connected at their south ends by a wagon traverser until 1972. There was an underground nuclear bunker nearby. (R.Geach)

5. SWANSEA VALE LINE

The Swansea Vale Railway opened for freight between the docks at Swansea and some collieries near Glais in 1815. Extension north to Pontardawe took place in 1859 and to Ystralyfera in 1861. Gwys and the terminus at Brynamman were reached in 1864. Horse power was changed to steam by 1860.

The SVR passenger service began between Swansea and Glais on 21st February 1860. Ystralyfera was reached on 20th November 1861 and service was extended to Brynamman on 2nd March 1868. The line between Upper Bank and Morriston came into use on 2nd October 1871 and it was extended north to Glais in March 1871, carrying passengers from the outset.

The SVR became part of the Midland Railway in 1876 and this was incorporated into the LMSR in 1923. The Morriston Loop and the route to Brynamman lost passenger trains on 25th September 1950.

Passenger Services:

There was an occasional extra train south of Ystralyfera in the early years, this rising to four in the later years, but weekdays only.

	Weekdays	Sundays
1865	3	2
1870	2	2
1894	4	0
1920	7	0
1949	4	0

BRYNAMMAN

5a. The 1908 edition has the MR line from Swansea on the right and the left one is annotated. Centre is **Stations** as each company had their own, linked by a freight connection.

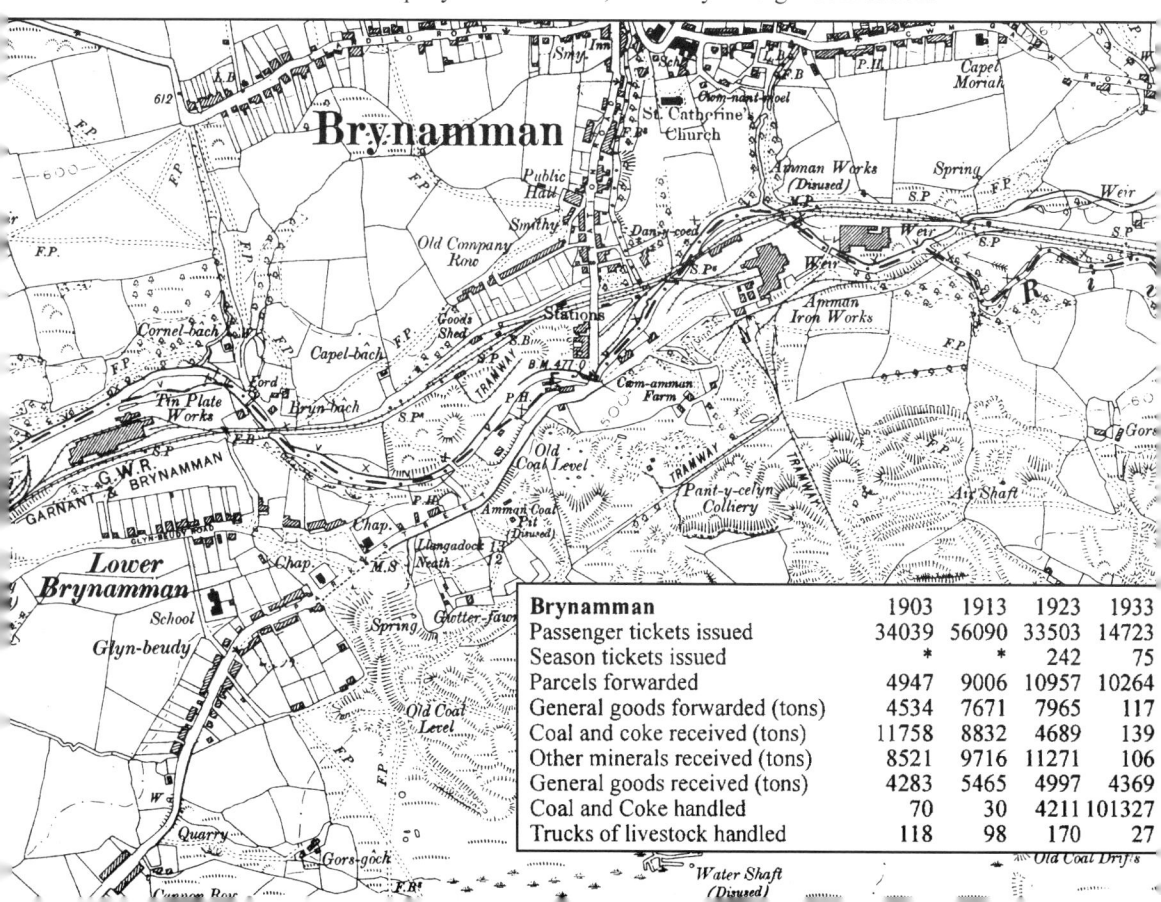

Brynamman	1903	1913	1923	1933
Passenger tickets issued	34039	56090	33503	14723
Season tickets issued	*	*	242	75
Parcels forwarded	4947	9006	10957	10264
General goods forwarded (tons)	4534	7671	7965	117
Coal and coke received (tons)	11758	8832	4689	139
Other minerals received (tons)	8521	9716	11271	106
General goods received (tons)	4283	5465	4997	4369
Coal and Coke handled	70	30	4211	101327
Trucks of livestock handled	118	98	170	27

5.1 The first two pictures illustrate the ex-GWR terminus on 27th April 1948. This shows 0-6-0PT no. 3752 propelling the coaches of the 11.15am from Llanelly into the loop prior to running round them. Other coaches stand on the goods shed road; freight continued until 28th September 1964, via the ex-MR route. Passenger traffic ceased on 18th August 1958 and the 28-lever signal box closed. (H.C.Casserley)

5.2 We look under the loading gauge at a train upon arrival. It is signalled to reverse into the loop. The suffix WEST was used from January 1950. The station was supervised from the ex-LMS one from 1st August 1929. Until then, the GWR had a staff numbering 10 or 12. (H.C.Casserley)

5.3 Two more photographs from the same day present the ex-MR station. 0-6-0T no. 7481 waits to propel the 11.36am to Swansea St. Thomas. (H.C.Casserley)

5.4 The driving end of the same train is seen along with the small bridge under Station Road. Its limited width prohibited the passage of coaching stock. The track on the right is to the ex-GWR station. (Lens of Sutton coll.)

5.5 The skew bridge over the River Amman was photographed in 1961, along with the connection to the ex-GWR station at the end of it. The ex-MR station building is beyond the signal post and was termed EAST from January 1950 until passenger service withdrawal on 25th September 1950. The line on the bridge on the left served a brickworks until 31st May 1964. (R.J.Essery/R.S.Carpenter)

5.6   The date is 15th September 1962 and the SLS tour DMU waited here whilst some tour participants chose to leave the train and walk to West Goods. It ran from Aberavon Town to Swansea High Street. The 28-lever box was open until 27th September 1964. (G.Adams/M.J.Stretton coll.)

CWMLLYNFELL

5.7   This stop opened on 1st July 1909 and lasted to the end. It had earlier served as Gwaun-Cae-Gurwen Colliery Halt, opening on 7th December 1896 for colliers only. The left signal is for the loop from which the colliery line diverged from 1899 to 1964. To the north was GCG Sidings Box until 27th February 1964. (P.Laming coll.)

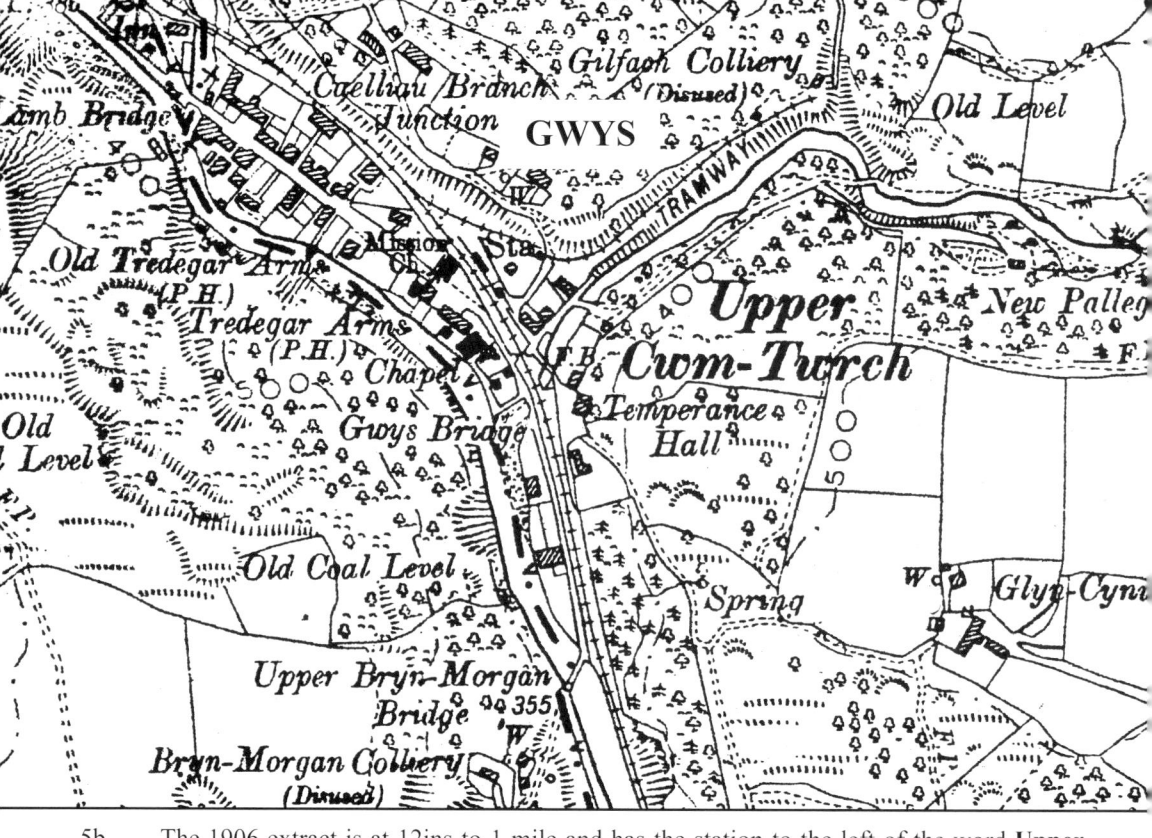

5b. The 1906 extract is at 12ins to 1 mile and has the station to the left of the word **Upper**. Further north is the junction for the Caelliau Branch, which was in use from 1874 to 1962, serving Brynllynfell Colliery, Brynhenllys Colliery and Black Mountain Colliery.

5.8 A northward panorama shows the scene five years after the last passenger had left. The goods yard remained open until 1st April 1963. Nearby were Blaen Cwm Colliery sidings from 1908 to 1956. (M.Hale)

SOUTH OF GWYS

5.9   The engine shed at Gurnos was built in 1900 and is below the word **Gurnos** on map 5c. No. 47481 is seen in 1952; closure was on 2nd April 1962. (M.Whitehouse coll.)

5c.   The 1900 edition has the N&BR lower right. There were 32 private sidings listed under Gurnos in 1938. The public sidings were in use until 12th July 1965. Opened in 1906, they were east of the engine shed. Ystalyfera station is lower left and it had its own goods yard until November 1927.

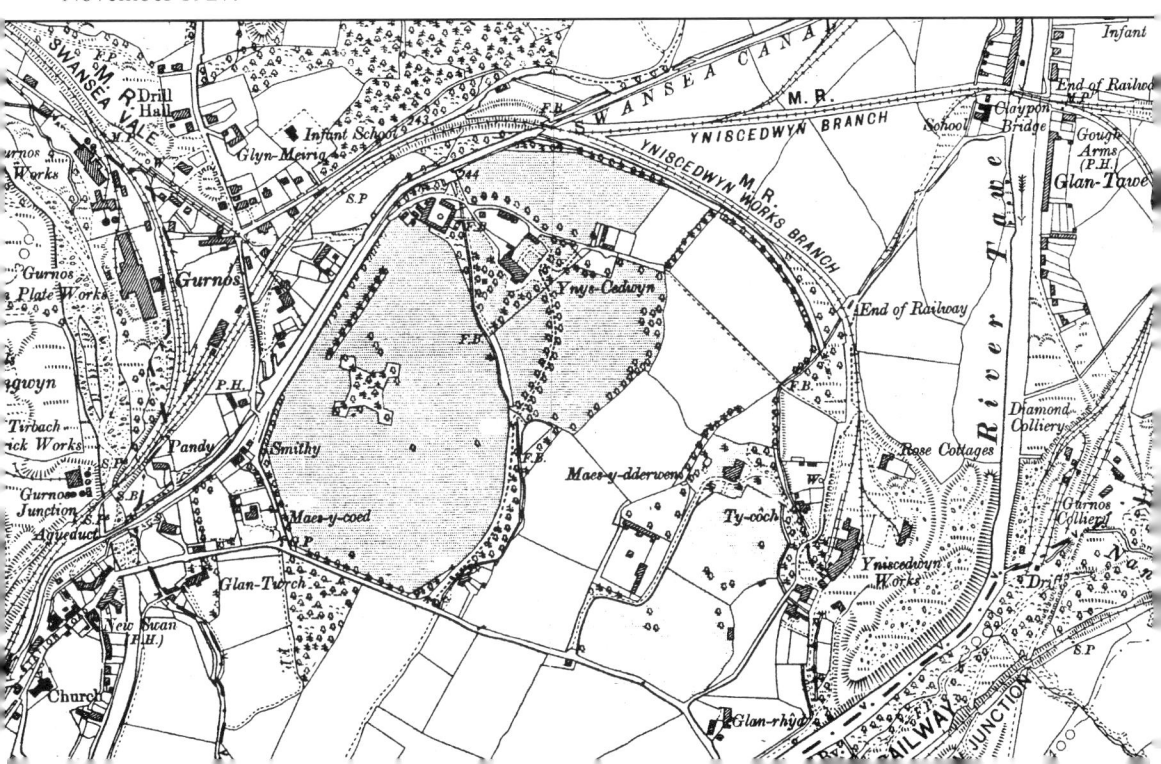

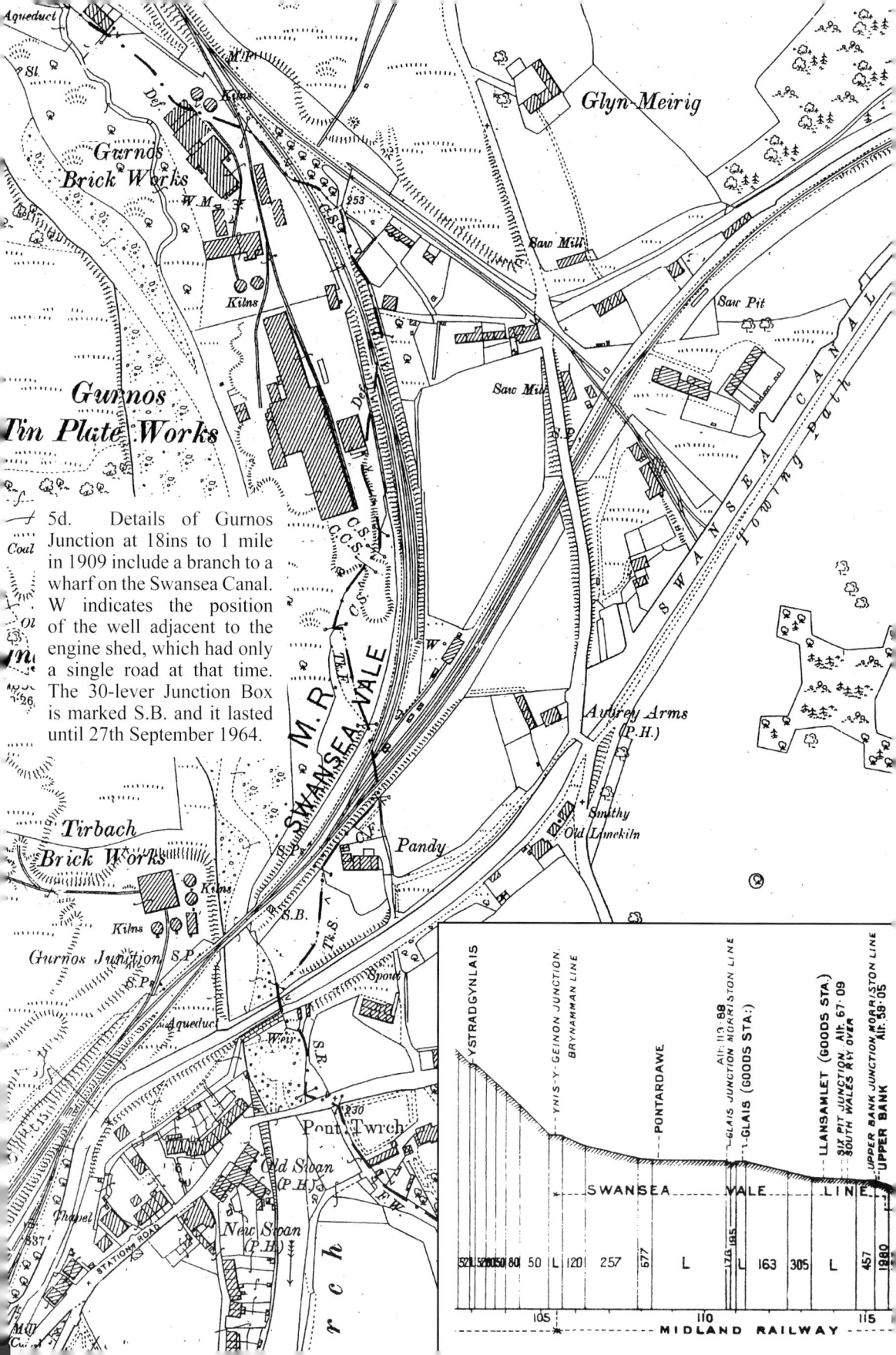

5d. Details of Gurnos Junction at 18ins to 1 mile in 1909 include a branch to a wharf on the Swansea Canal. W indicates the position of the well adjacent to the engine shed, which had only a single road at that time. The 30-lever Junction Box is marked S.B. and it lasted until 27th September 1964.

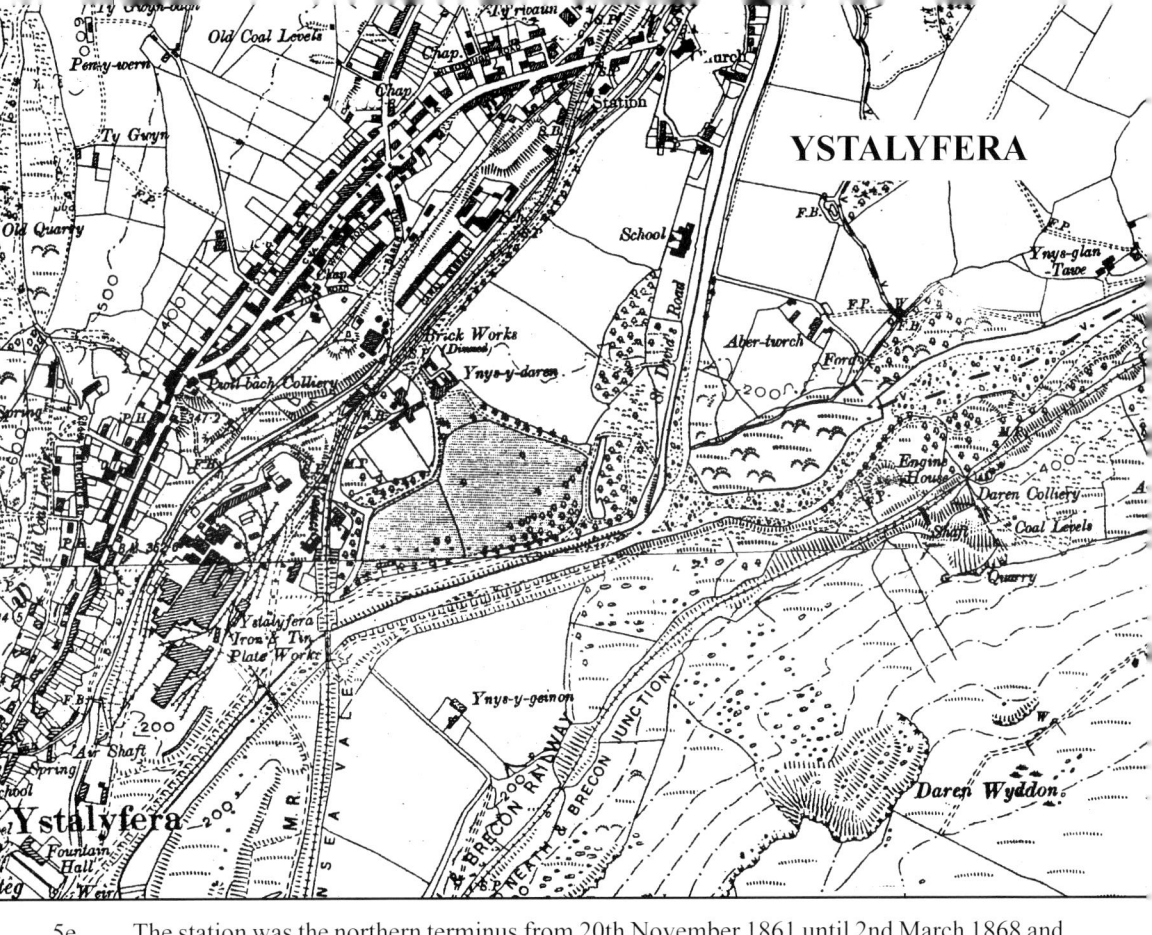

5e.   The station was the northern terminus from 20th November 1861 until 2nd March 1868 and is near the top of this 1900 extract. The town had a population of 4720 in 1961.

5.10   An undated postcard shows the Pwllbach Colliery line on the left. It had formed a loop for many years and lasted until 27th September 1964. There was a 24-lever signal box until 1956. (P.Laming coll.)

SOUTH OF YSTALYFERA

5.11 **YNISGEINON JUNCTION** is the name on the box and its 20-lever frame was in use until 20th February 1967, when the line from Brecon closed. (R.S.Carpenter)

5.12 It is 15th September 1962 and the SLS "Swansea Area Railtour No. 1" was in progress. The Brecon line is the centre one; the train is on a loop which joins it. (G.Adams/M.J.Stretton coll.)

PONTARDAWE

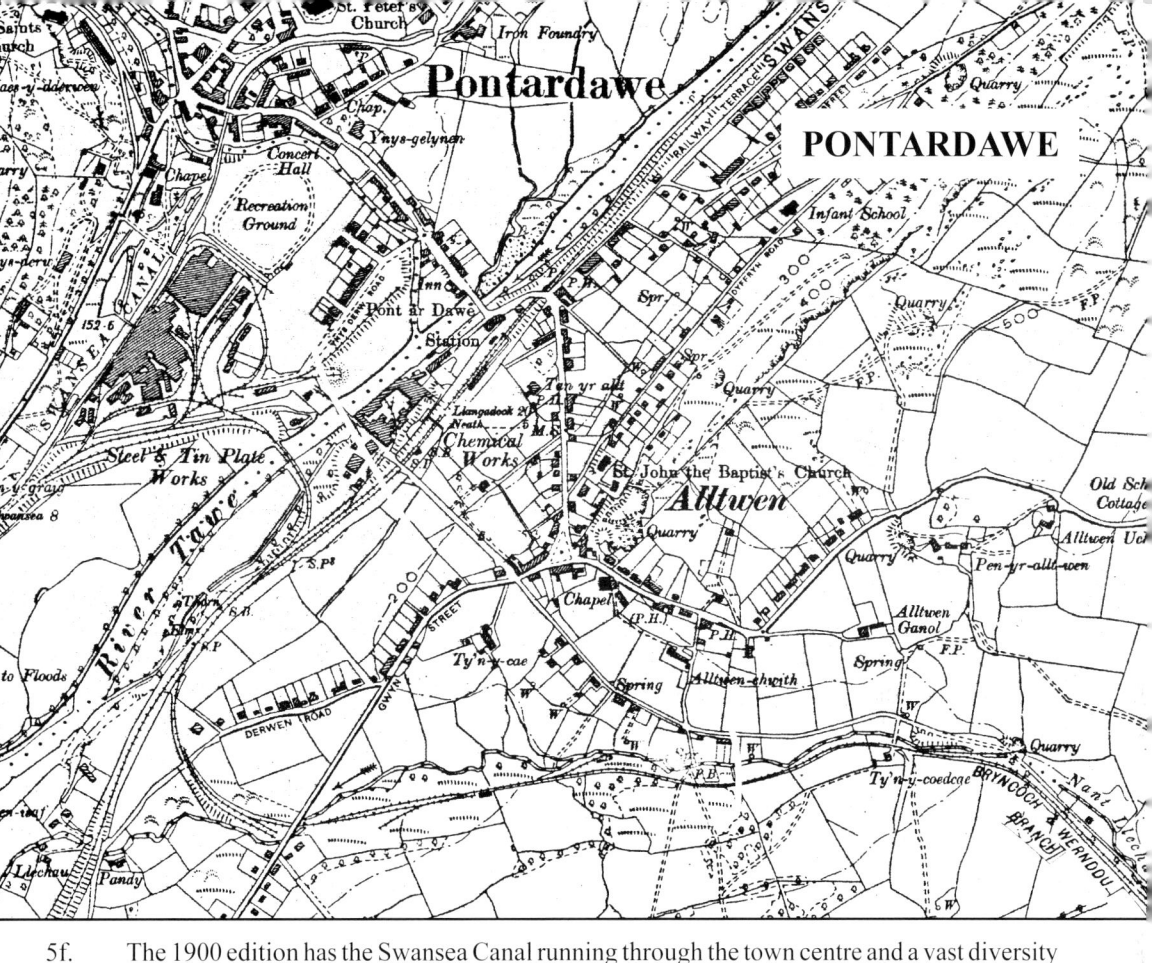

5f. The 1900 edition has the Swansea Canal running through the town centre and a vast diversity of businesses around it. The line on the right served three collieries, plus a brickworks and was in use from 1893 to 1936. It was a private siding.

5.13 A view north in 1906 includes North Box, which closed on 12th May 1929. Behind the camera is Station Box, which served until 7th November 1965. The goods shed is evident; the yard was in use until 22nd April 1964. It had a 3-ton crane. (LGRP)

GLAIS

5.14   The simple station faced north and had a tramway pass under the line beyond its east end. Goods traffic continued until 8th November 1965. (P.Laming coll.)

5g.   The 1900 survey shows the station to be on the route to Morriston, which is on the left. Its predecessor is shown as *Goods Sta*. The transition took place on 1st March 1875 when the route south lost its passenger service and the stations at Birchgrove and Llansamlet were closed.

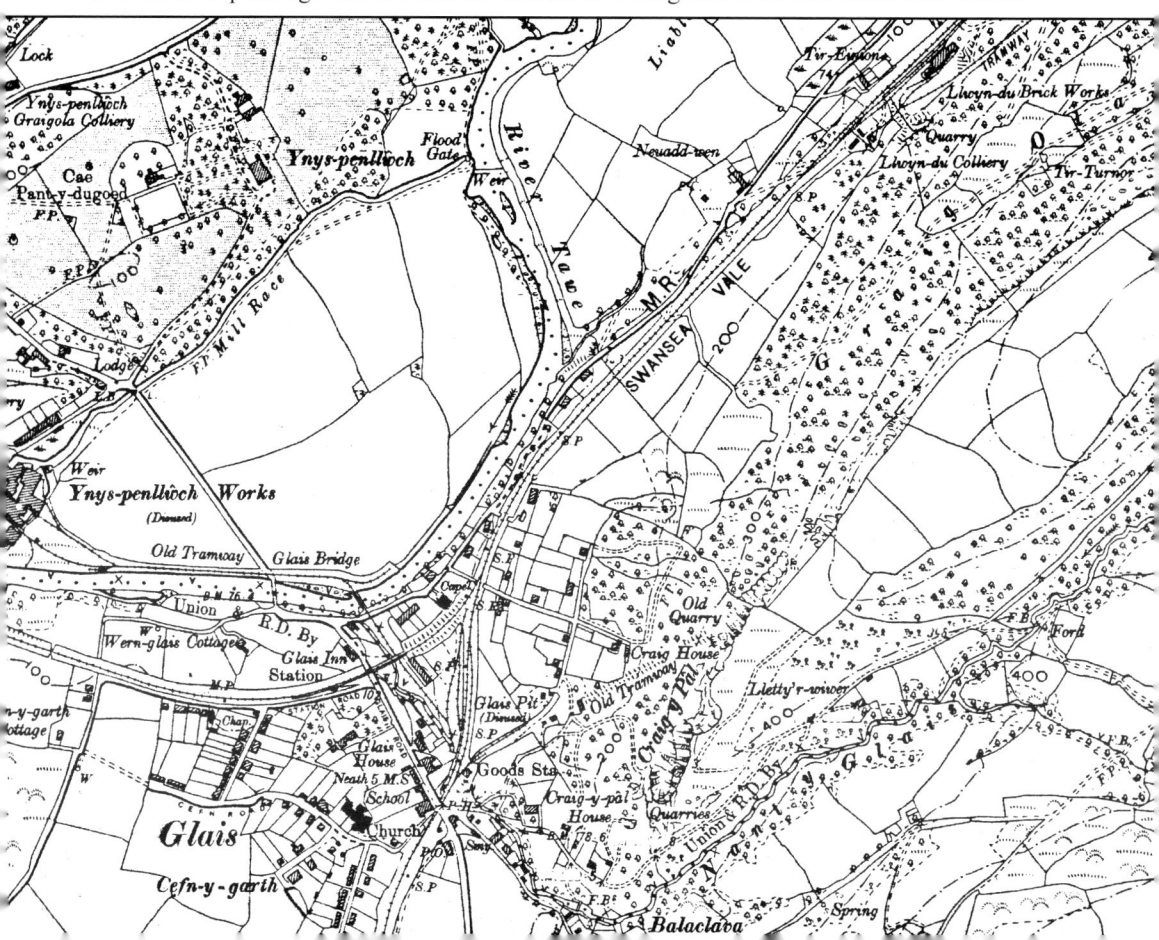

CLYDACH-ON-TAWE

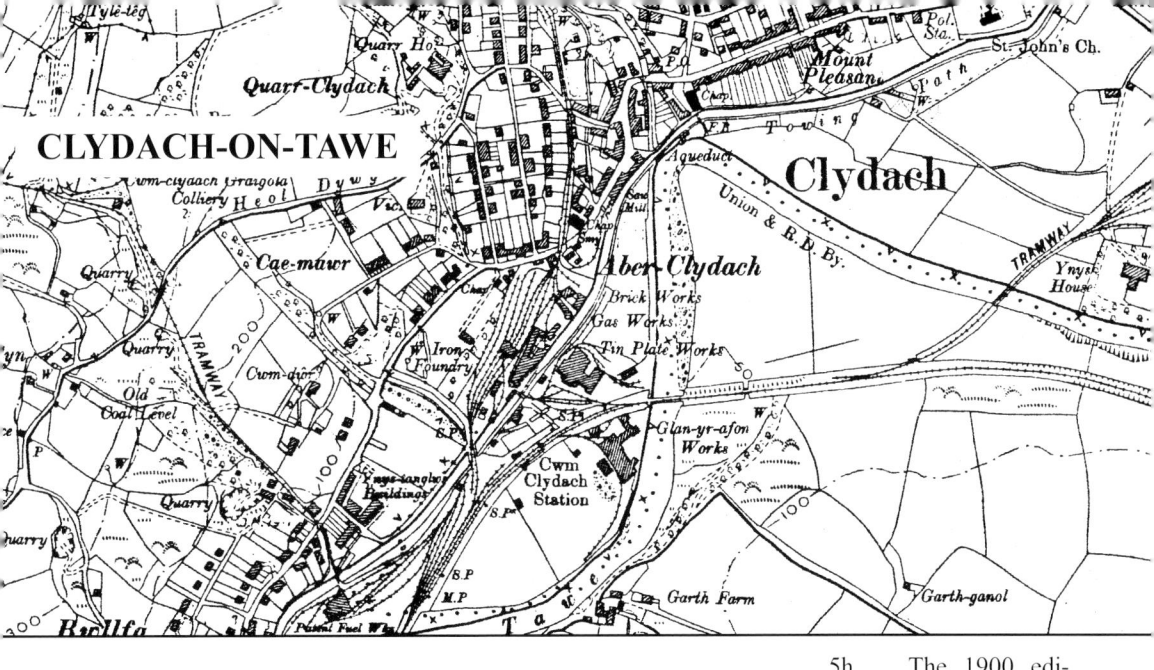

5h. The 1900 edition has the stations original name; it was changed on 1st October 1901. It had eleven private sidings listed in 1938 and several of them are shown here.

5.15 We look west at the modern station, which was well lit and had good telephone provision. In the background is Graigola Merthyr Fuel Works, which had its own siding until 1956. (P.Laming coll.)

5.16 Clydach Merthyr Colliery was photographed in 1918. It had opened in 1863 and in 1954, 523 men produced 115,571 tons of coal. Closure came in June 1961. The line to it is at the top of the map. (Unknown)

5.17 A view in the other direction completes our study of the station. Prominent is Glanyrafon Tin Plate Works, which had a siding from 1880 until 1952. The line south to Morriston closed on 1st September 1965. (P.Laming coll.)

5.18 There is now no trace of the railway, as it had been lost under a roundabout. On 8th October 1983, the MRS "The Coed Bach Connection" railtour stopped to allow participants to explore the remnants. It had run from Felin Fran; this line served the Mond Works until 1992 and was ex-GWR, not part of the former MR. (D.H.Mitchell)

MORRISTON EAST

5i. The station opened as the terminus of the line from Swansea on 2nd October 1871 and became a through station in March 1895. The suffix EAST was used from January 1950, but closure came on 25th September 1950. It is shown just below Wychtree Bridge on the 1900 map.

5.19   This is a southward panorama from the bridge in 1961, with shunting at the steel works in progress. Its sidings lasted until 12th May 1972 and the line south closed on 24th May 1983, when few industries needed it. South Box is in the distance; it had 24 levers and closed on 22nd February 1965. North Box had 16 and lasted until 13th February 1956. (Stations UK)

5.20   The neglected buildings are seen in 1962 as 0-6-0PT no. 6741 runs through. The local goods yard had a 6-ton crane and lasted until 4th October 1965. There were an amazing 23 private sidings here in 1938. (D.K.Jones)

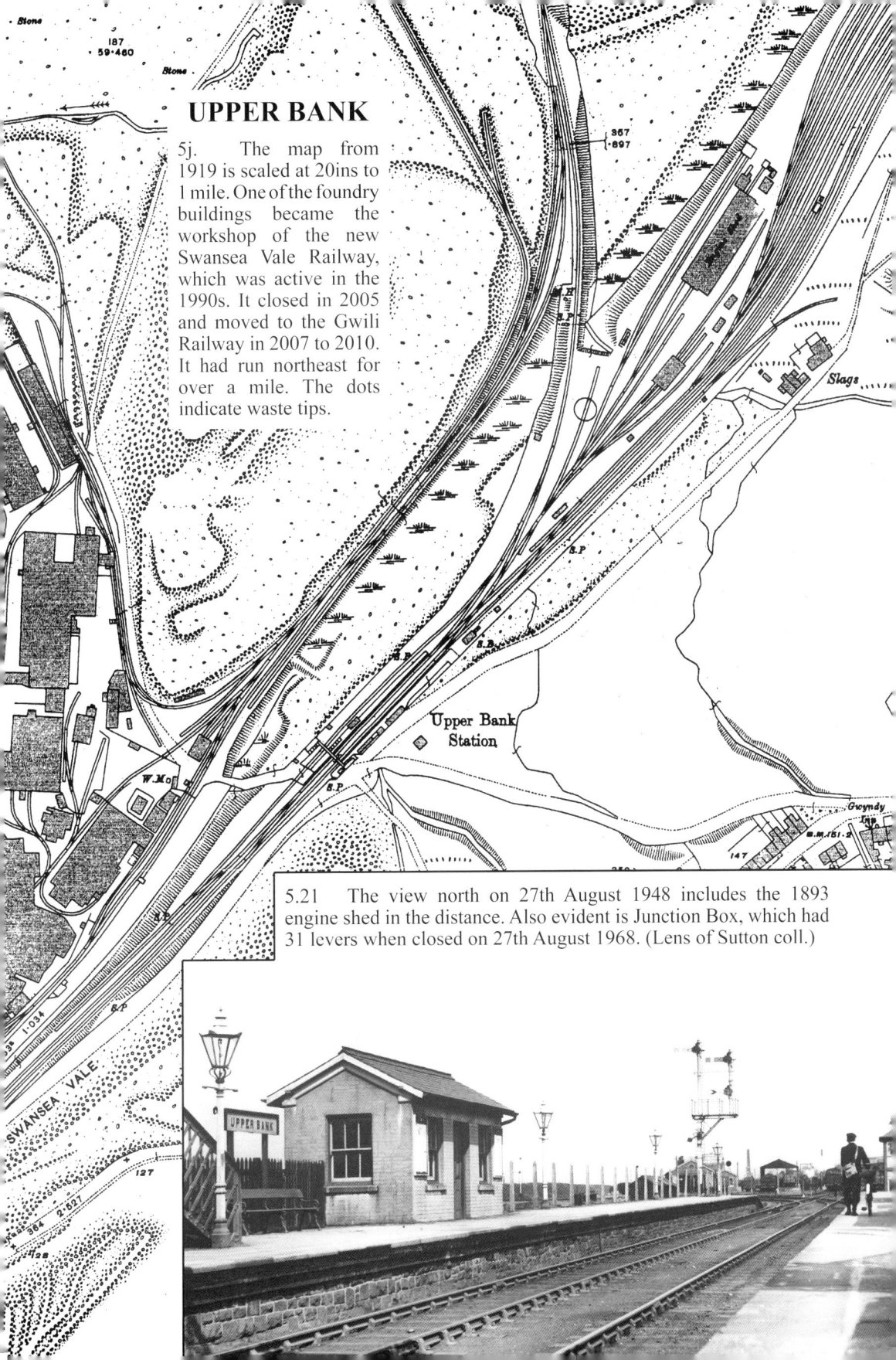

UPPER BANK

5j. The map from 1919 is scaled at 20ins to 1 mile. One of the foundry buildings became the workshop of the new Swansea Vale Railway, which was active in the 1990s. It closed in 2005 and moved to the Gwili Railway in 2007 to 2010. It had run northeast for over a mile. The dots indicate waste tips.

5.21 The view north on 27th August 1948 includes the 1893 engine shed in the distance. Also evident is Junction Box, which had 31 levers when closed on 27th August 1968. (Lens of Sutton coll.)

5.22   On the right in this photograph from 13th June 1954 is the coal stage, the raised siding reducing the manual effort for those with shovels. The shed code was 4C in 1948 and 1949 and 87K sub thereafter. In 1954 there were 13 tank engines based here. It closed in 1963. (P.Glenn/R.S.Carpenter)

5.23   Another picture from the 1950s and this is from the level crossing, with the ground frame on the right. There was a third line over the road beyond the gate on the left. (H.C.Casserley)

SWANSEA
ST. THOMAS

k. North Dock Goods Branch
s shown crossing New Cut on a
rawbridge, on the 1900 survey. It
iverges from the MR on the curve,
ut only the S of SB shows. Lower
own is the MR terminus, St. Thomas,
nd to the left of it is the other New
ut Bridge, which was initially a
rawbridge, but became a swing
ridge in about 1900. The curve from
he north to the east is not clear.

Dock opening dates:

North Dock	1852
South Dock	1859
PoW Dock	1882
Kings Dock	1909
Queens Dock	1920

5.24 Harbour Branch Box had 40 levers and closed on 7th May 1967. These three pictures are from Spring 1966. There had been a fourth track near to the box until 1964.
(C.Jones)

5.25 The class 08 diesel is taking empties to Morriston East, having run from the sidings in the background. Those on the left were used for wagon repairs.
(C.Jones)

5.26 Another view from the signal box and this features empties bound for Ynyscedwyn Colliery. The New Cut drawbridge was taken out of railway use on 7th November 1954. The line to Upper Bank was singled on 27th May 1968 and closed on 28th October 1969.
(C.Jones)

5.27   This southward view of North Dock has the VofNR viaduct to Wind Street Junction feint in the left background and mixed gauge track in the foreground. The wide buffers on the engine allowed it to move wagons of either gauge. The wagons behind it are broad gauge and each carries four containers. Wind is to turn, not a breeze. (GWR)

5.28   The exterior of St. Thomas Station was photographed in about 1900. The buildings were destroyed soon after closure on 25th September 1950. (Unknown)

5.29 A train for Brynamman waits to depart behind 0-6-0T no. 7481 on 27th August 1948. The signal in the background is on the East Dock to South Dock viaduct line. (H.C.Casserley)

5.30 The same train was recorded minutes later, the flaking paint being more obvious. The signal box never carried the name of the station; its 24-lever frame was in use until 27th May 1968. Sidings were laid over the station area in 1961. (H.C.Casserley)

5.31 A 1955 view of a railtour includes the short canopy, plus facilities for gentlemen, still available five years after closure. (Stations UK)

6. MORRISTON BRANCH

This was opened between Landore and Morriston on 9th May 1881, by the GWR. It ran almost parallel to the 1875 route of the Midland's SVR. The GWR extended north in 1914, to provide a link with its new Swansea District Line, detailed in Section 7. Trains could run through to the halt and extensive sidings at Felin Fran.

A line north from here to Clydach was completed by 1922 and it was extended to Trebanos in 1923. The former had a public goods yard until 12th July 1965. A mile north of the latter was Daren Colliery, which used the sidings until its closure in 1964. It was originally known as Graig Colliery and it had an aerial ropeway to the MR initially. The connection to Abernant was begun, but never completed.

The route was closed to passengers on 11th June 1956 and singled on 29th January 1962. Total closure came in 1965.

Passenger Services:

Trains ran on weekdays and conveyed many railway workers to Felin Fran Yard after 1914. The frequency samples are: 1882-3, 1902-2, 1922-4, 1937-12 and 1948-1. There were extras south of Morriston on Saturdays in the early years.

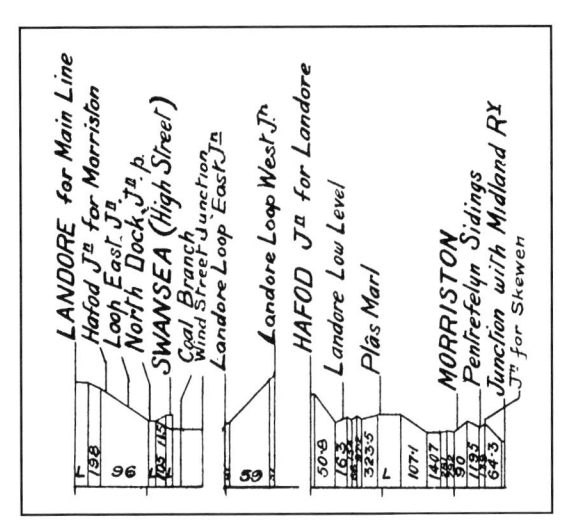

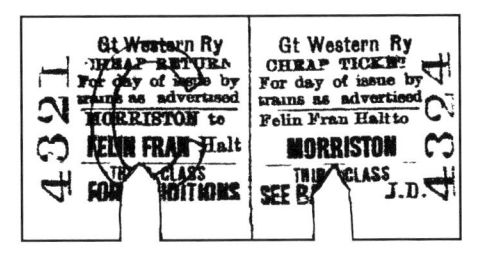

FELIN FRAN HALT

6.1   Our journey starts at a remote location due to the incomplete nature of the route. This view west is from 27th August 1959. The halt was open from 21st January 1922 to 11th June 1956. The staff numbered around 35 for most of the 1930s, all being involved with freight traffic. (M.Hale)

6.2   At their optimum, there were eight through sidings north of the four running lines and seven to the south. Decline set in and four can be seen south of the two tracks of the Swansea District Line on 8th October 1983, as no. 37177 departs. (D.H.Mitchell)

PENTREFELIN (GLAM) HALT

6.3   The wooden framed platforms were recorded on 27th August 1959. The halt opened on 16th April 1928. This view north includes the 24-lever box, which closed on 29th January 1962. (M.Hale)

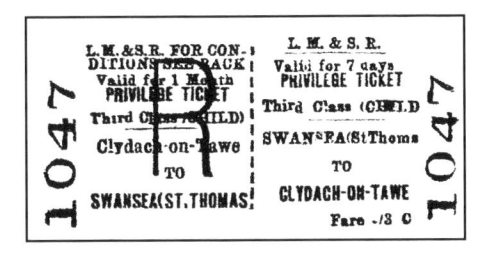

MORRISTON WEST

6.4 The station location is shown on map 5i in 1900. This southward panorama is from 1961, five years after the last passenger had left. Goods traffic continued here until about 1964. WEST was added in 1950. (Stations UK)

6.5 This was the terminus from 9th May 1881 until about 1915. The signal box had 34 levers and was in use until 4th October 1965. The number of residents had grown to over 10,000 by that time. The staff numbered six in 1903 and nine in 1930. (Lens of Sutton coll.)

COPPER PIT PLATFORM

6.6   The stop was introduced in February 1915 and was close to Copper Pit Colliery, which can be found at the bottom of map 5i. This had its own siding from 1909 to 1932. This southward view is from 1961 and the Swansea Canal is on the left. (Stations UK)

6.7   Here we look north in about 1965. South of here was Spelter Works Loop, which had a signal box from 1915 to 1928. The sidings lasted until 1964. (Lens of Sutton coll.)

PLAS MARL

6.8 This stop opened with the line. The box and a loop came into use on 12th December 1915. The former became a ground frame on 13th June 1928, when the latter was taken out of use. (Lens of Sutton coll.)

→ 6a. Plas Marl station is shown above centre on this 1900 map and thus Landore appears without its triangular junction. Upper Bank is seen again, lower right.

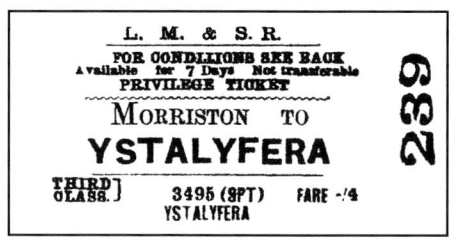

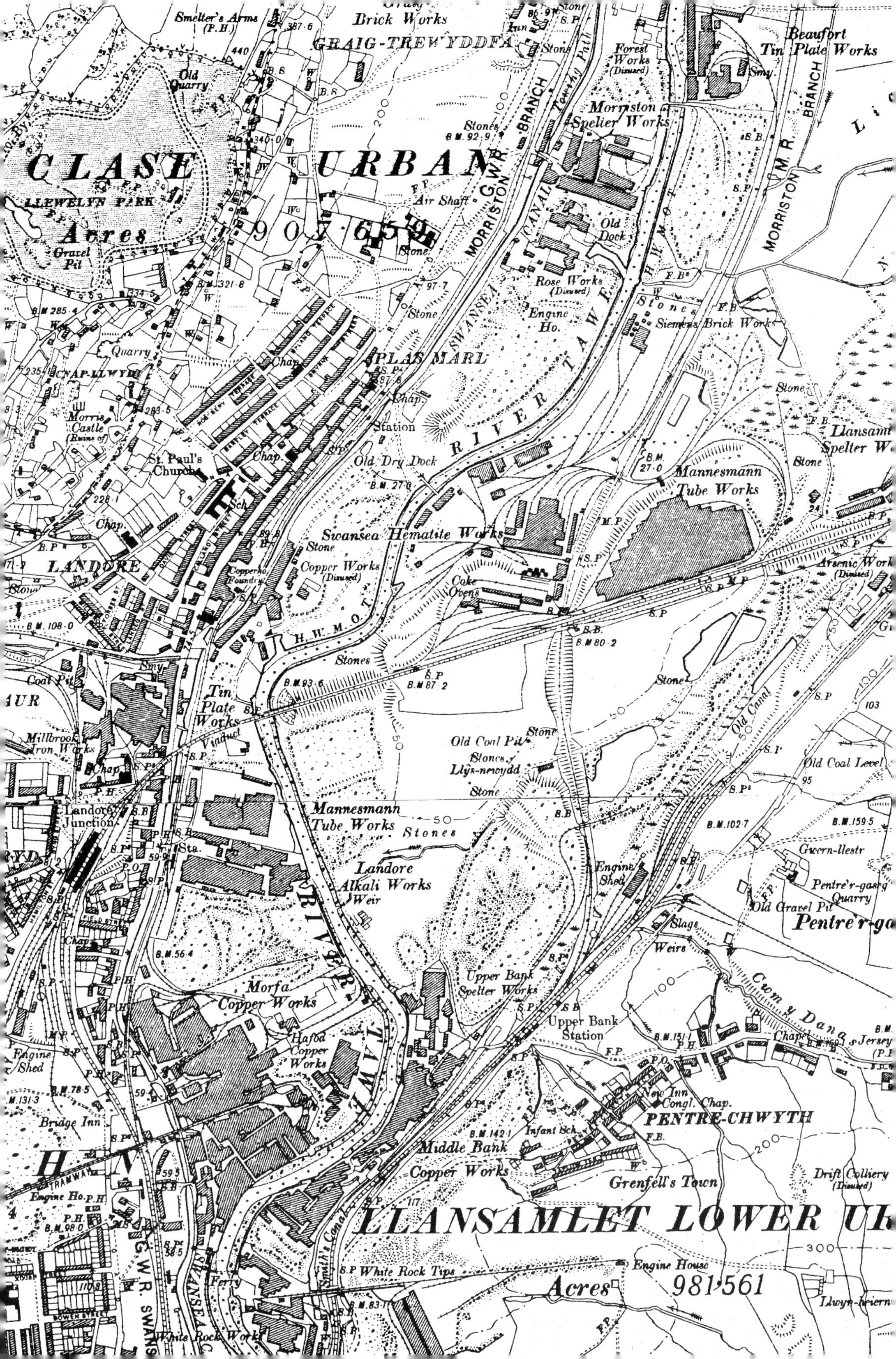
Smelter's Arms (P.H.)
Brick Works
GRAIG-TREWYDDFA
Beaufort Tin Plate Works
Forest Works (Disused)
Morriston Spelter Works
Old Quarry
CLASE URBAN
LLEWELYN PARK
Acres
907.659
Gravel Pit
Air Shaft
Stone
MORRISTON G.W.R. BRANCH
MORRISTON M.R. BRANCH
SWANSEA CANAL
Old Dock
Rose Works (Disused)
Engine Ho.
Siemens Brick Works
Quarry
CNAP-LLWYD
Morris Castle (Ruins of)
PLAS MARL
Station
Chap.
RIVER TAWE
St. Paul's Church
Sch.
Old Dry Dock
Llansamlet Spelter W
Mannesmann Tube Works
Swansea Hematite Works
LANDORE
Copper Works (Disused)
Coke Ovens
Arsenic Work (Disused)
Stones
Coal Pit
Tin Plate Works
Viaduct
Millbrook Iron Works
Old Coal Pit
Stones
Llys-newydd
Old Canal
Old Coal Level
Landore Junction
Sta.
Mannesmann Tube Works
Landore Alkali Works
Weir
Engine Shed
Gwern-llestr
Pentre'r-gasg Quarry
Old Gravel Pit
Pentre'r-ga
Slags
Weirs
Cwm y Danas
Morfa Copper Works
Upper Bank Spelter Works
Upper Bank Station
Hafod Copper Works
Engine Shed
Chapel
Jersey
New Inn
Congl. Chap.
PENTRE-CHWYTH
Bridge Inn
Infant Sch.
Middle Bank Copper Works
Grenfell's Town
Drift Colliery (Disused)
TRAMWAY
Engine Ho.
LLANSAMLET LOWER UR
Smith's Canal
G.W.R. SWANS
SWANSEA C
White Rock Tips
Engine House
Ferry
Acres
981.561
Llwyn-brian
White Rock Works

LANDORE LOW LEVEL

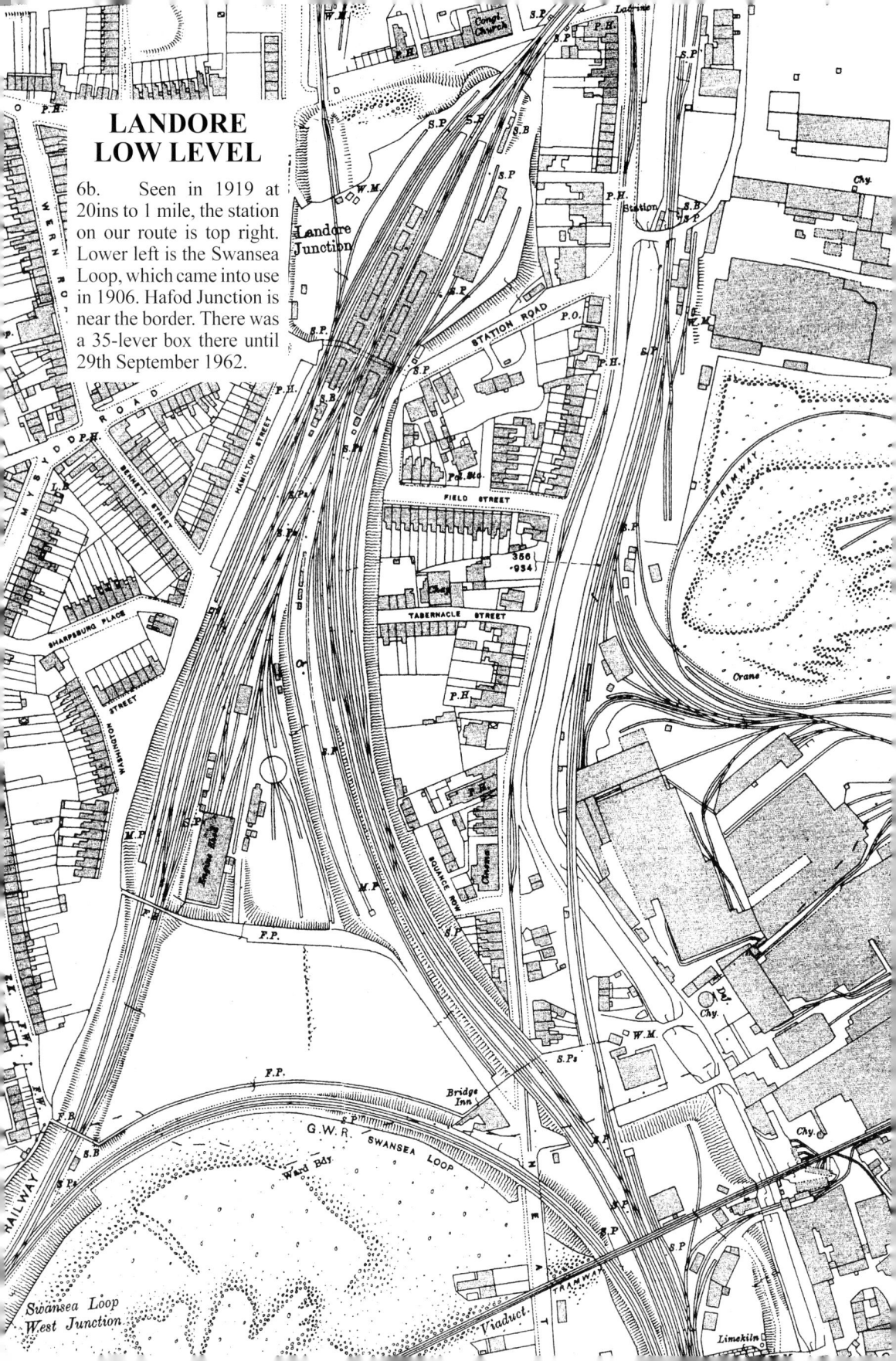

6b. Seen in 1919 at 20ins to 1 mile, the station on our route is top right. Lower left is the Swansea Loop, which came into use in 1906. Hafod Junction is near the border. There was a 35-lever box there until 29th September 1962.

6.9   We look south in about 1935, but cannot see the chemical works siding, which was in use until 1963. The signal box had 16 levers and probably closed at that time. There were 17 men here in 1913 and 26 in 1923. Low Level closed on 6th January 1954. (Stations UK)

6.10   A view in the other direction in 1964 features the main line to Cardiff climbing over the Tawe Valley. Most trains reversed at High Street (or made connections there) after 1964, when the former High Level closed. The viaduct was realigned and rebuilt in 1978-1979. (Stations UK)

6.11　A southward panorama in September 1963 is from our route and has the main lines to Swansea High Street on the right. Hafod Junction is in the distance, as is the bridge for a former industrial complex. Beyond them were extensive carriage sidings and several industrial ones. The tallest signal posts are on the route to Llanelly. (P.J.Garland/R.S.Carpenter)

6.12　Map 6b shows the extensive locomotive depot, which closed to steam in June 1961. The diesel depot on the site is seen on 14th May 1988, with two class 08 diesel shunters close to a snow plough. (P.Jones)

For views of Landore High Level and Swansea High Street, please see *Cardiff to Swansea* and *Swansea to Carmarthen*.

SWANSEA HIGH STREET

6.13   The first station had two platforms and two more were added on the west side in 1879, plus a short bay in 1897. There were electric trams in the streets of Swansea from 1900 to 1937. (P.Laming coll.)

6c.   A major rebuild took place in 1926-27 and this plan shows the arrangement in 1934. There were 129 men here that year and 261 in the goods depot. (Railway Magazine)

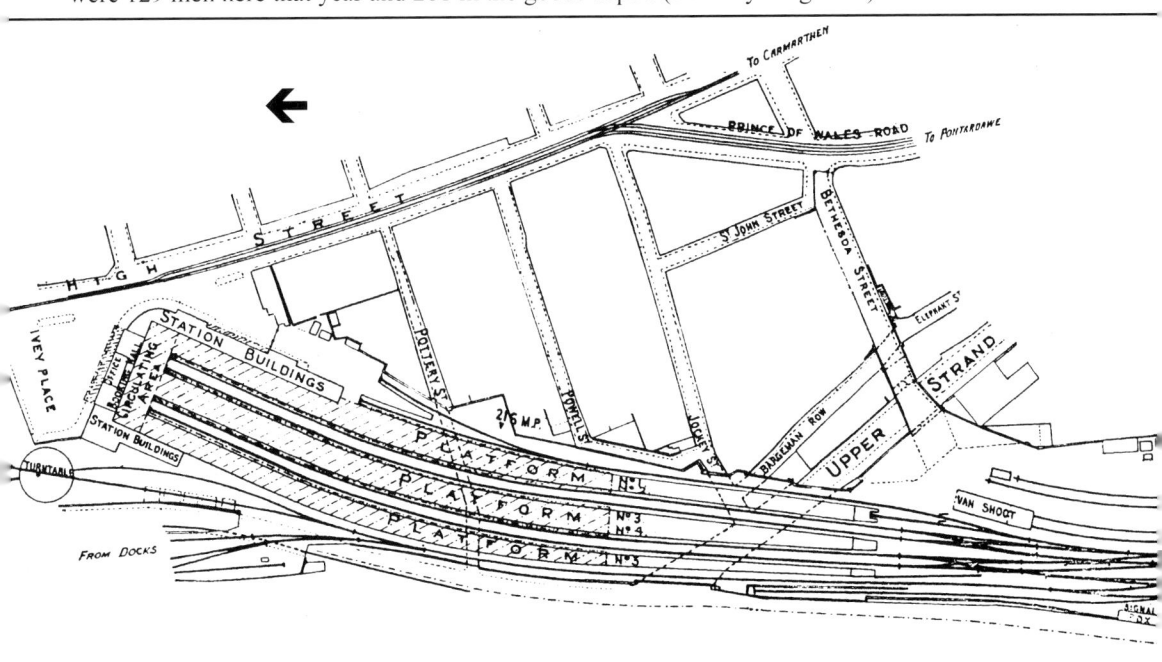

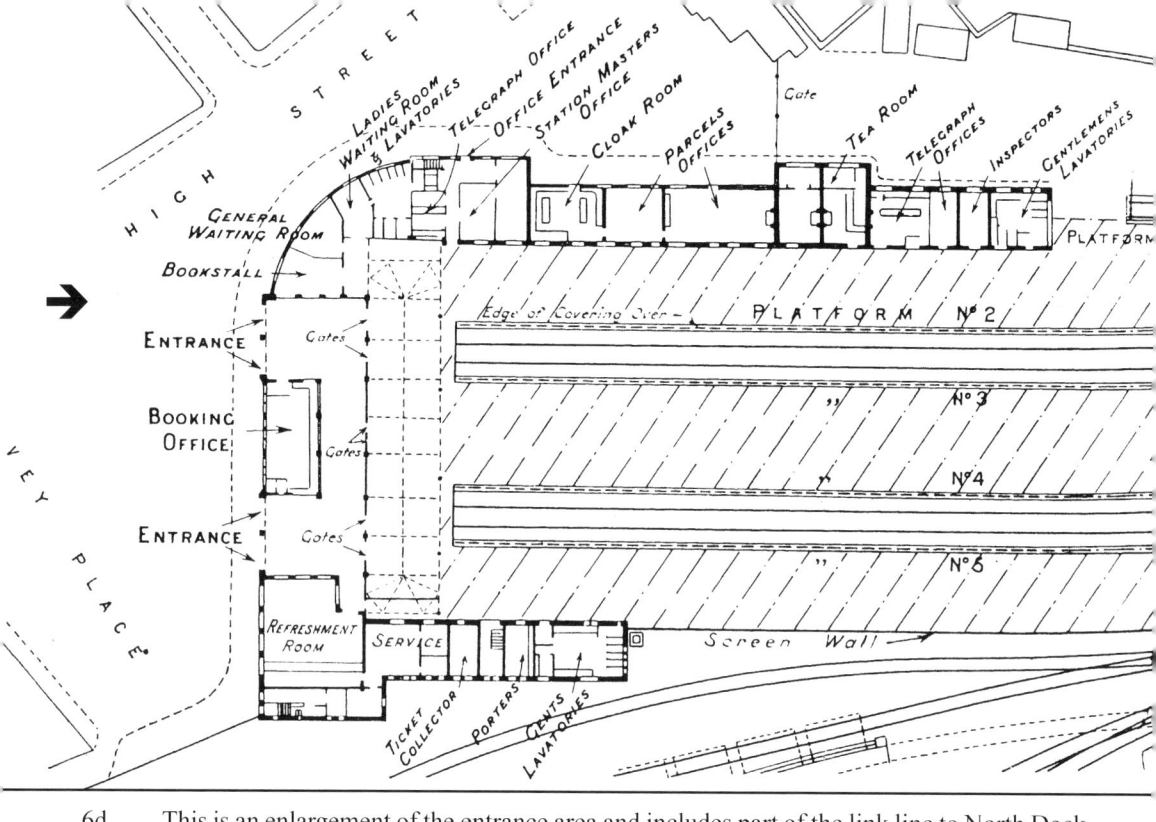

6d. This is an enlargement of the entrance area and includes part of the link line to North Dock. (Railway Magazine)

6.14 The south elevation of the 1927 building was recorded on a postcard and it remained little changed in the 21st century. (P.Laming coll.)

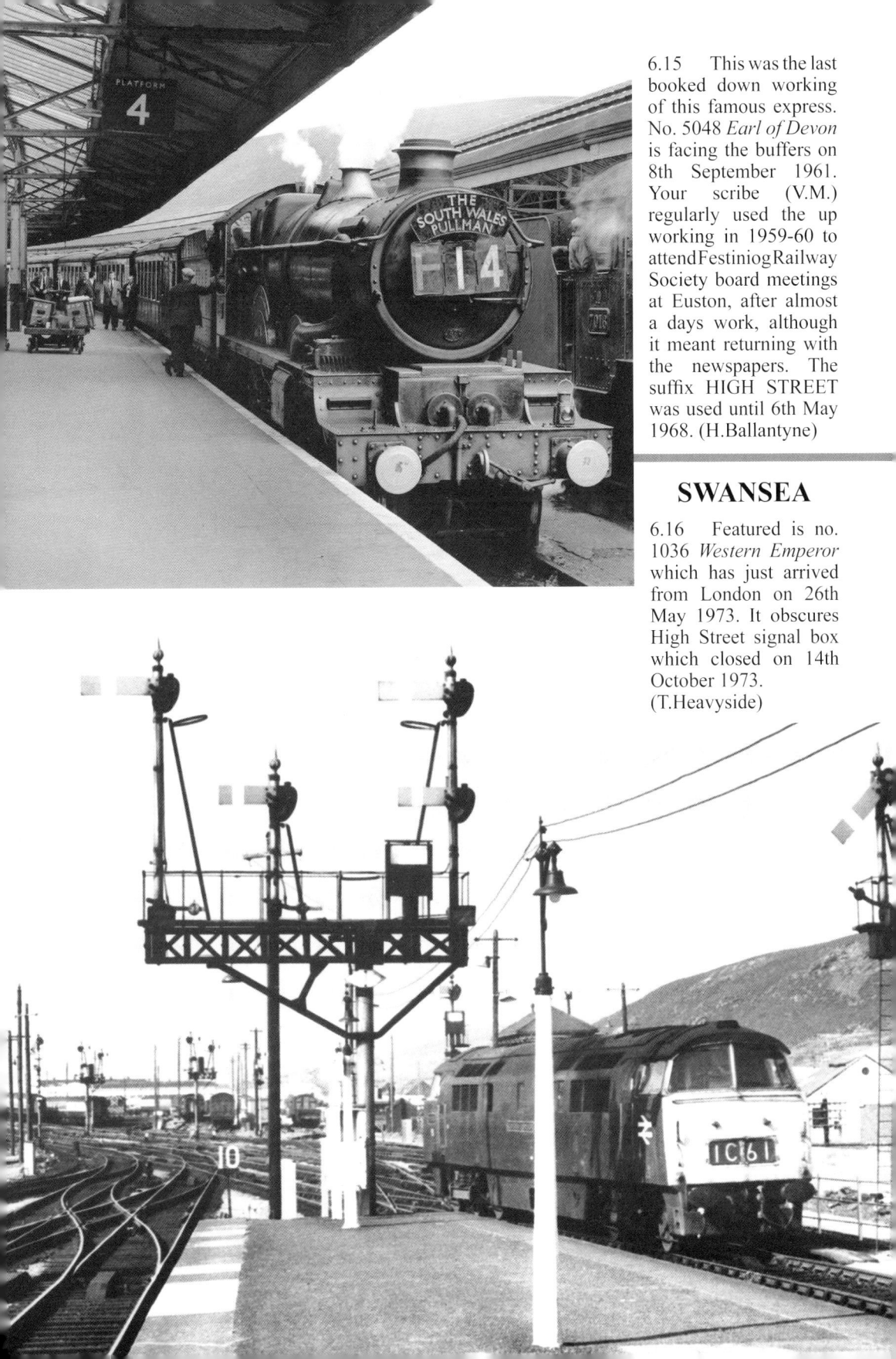

6.15 This was the last booked down working of this famous express. No. 5048 *Earl of Devon* is facing the buffers on 8th September 1961. Your scribe (V.M.) regularly used the up working in 1959-60 to attend Festiniog Railway Society board meetings at Euston, after almost a days work, although it meant returning with the newspapers. The suffix HIGH STREET was used until 6th May 1968. (H.Ballantyne)

SWANSEA

6.16 Featured is no. 1036 *Western Emperor* which has just arrived from London on 26th May 1973. It obscures High Street signal box which closed on 14th October 1973. (T.Heavyside)

6.17 When viewed from an HST on 25th July 2009 the area had lost the spoil heap and also the lines to North Dock and beyond, which had diverged on the left here, until closed on 8th November 1965. We are looking at platforms 3 and 4; they were renumbered on 14th October 1973, when the short no. 1 was lost. (V.Mitchell)

7. SWANSEA DISTRICT LINE

Early in 1910 the transatlantic liners of the Cunard Company began to omit their call at Queenstown in Ireland, and to put in instead at Fishguard, on their way to Liverpool, but it was short lived. The GWR decided on the construction of a new line in South Wales, which would cut out the heavy gradients in the vicinity. This would also provide a more direct and less congested route for the boat specials. The main traffic would be anthracite to the main docks. The main part of this new route opened on 14th July 1913. In order to cut out the diversion through Neath, running powers were obtained over the lines of the Rhondda & Swansea Bay Railway, which paralleled those of the GWR main line at the point where the latter turns northwards to reach Neath, and the existing connection between the two lines, at Court Sart, was used to give access to R&SB metals.

The R&SB swingbridge carried the trains for the new line across the River Neath two miles to the south of Neath. However, immediately beyond, at Dynevor Junction, the new line struck off westwards, with a connecting spur from Jersey Marine, on the R&SB and GWR lines, coming in at Jersey Marine North junction. After this the Avoiding Line picks up, at Lonlas Junction, a spur which has diverged to the south of the main line at Skewen, and then the avoiding line passes in a tunnel under the main line from the south to the north side, reaching the marshalling sidings at Felin Fran. From here it runs west to join the branch from Llanelly to Pontardulais, which brings it back to the main line. The route was authorised under an Act of 15th August 1904 and the Neath loop came into use on 19th May 1915. It is the upper part of the triangle on map 1a.

Passenger Services: During the 14 months that the stations were open, there were three trains on weekdays only calling at them. In addition to the regular Fishguard boat trains, there were Summer trains to and from Tenby over the route. The former were still running in 2012, albeit only once a day and from Cardiff, not London.

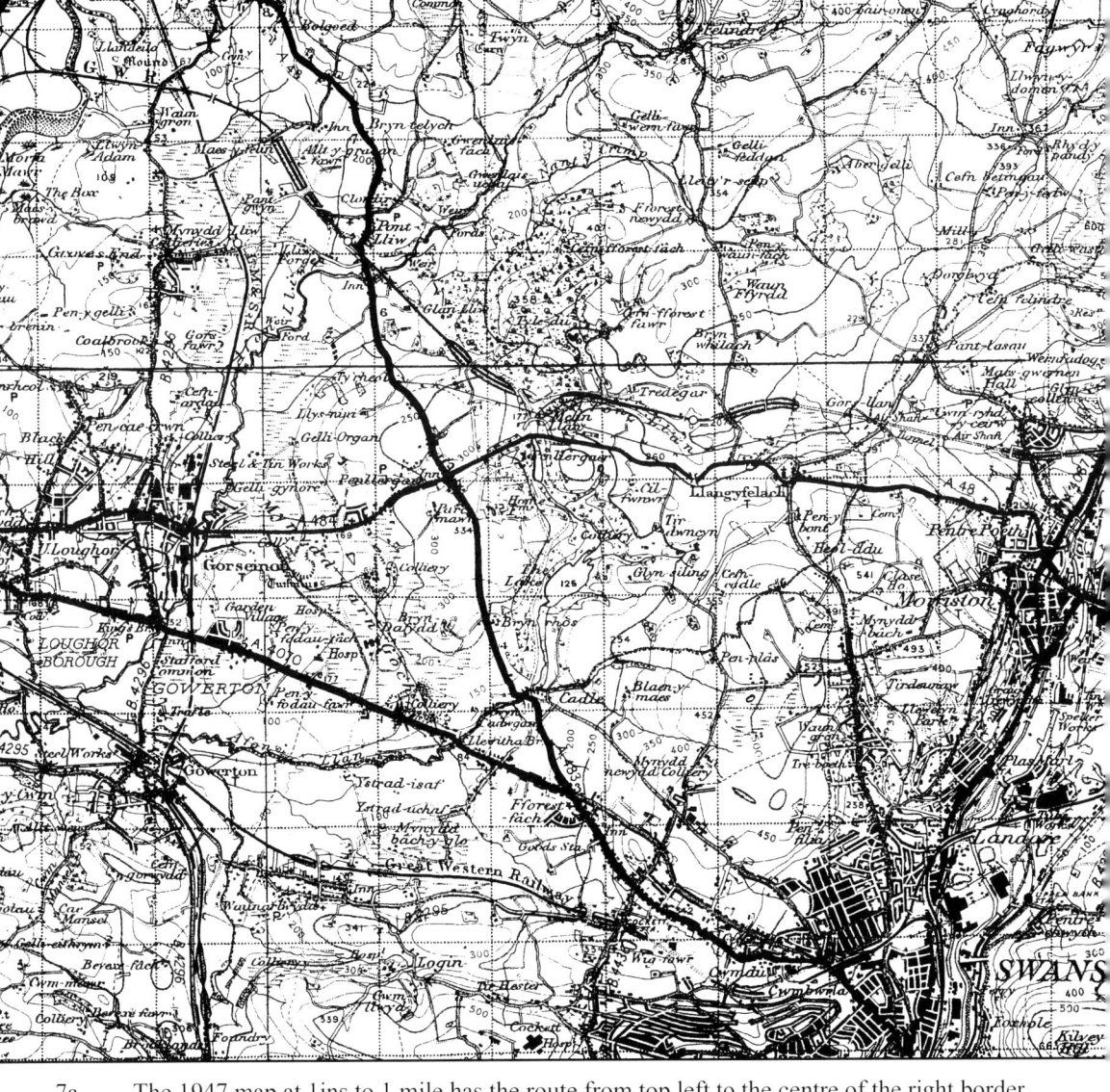

7a. The 1947 map at 1ins to 1 mile has the route from top left to the centre of the right border. The two closed stations are shown with open circles. Landore triangle is lower right.

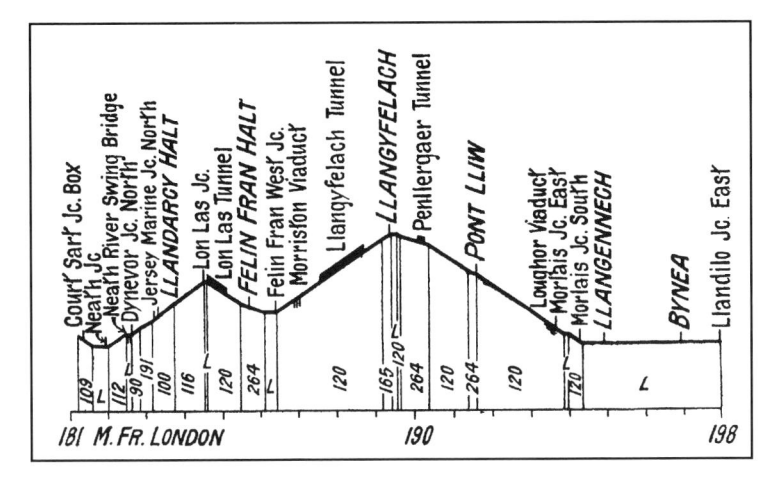

PONT LLIW

7.1   Both stations opened with the route and closed on 22nd September 1924. This one differed in having four tracks. The loops lasted until 22nd November 1967, when the 66-lever signal box closed. There were two colliery sidings, plus one to a brickworks. The goods yard closed on 4th January 1965. The staff numbered 13 in 1923 and 8 in 1930. Goods tonnage was 368,833 and 225,847 in those years. (M.Hale)

LLANGYFELACH

7.2   Both stations were photographed on 27th August 1958 and here we witness 4200 class 2-8-0T no. 5255 passing with a down freight on the up gradient. The box had 46 levers and was in use until 17th June 1973. There was a siding to Velindre Tinplate Works until 1959 and also one to Glynoch Colliery. The goods yard was in use until 1st February 1965 with a staff of seven in the early 1930s. East of this location is Llangyfelach Tunnel, which is 1952yds in length, and then Felin Fran is reached. (M.Hale)

8. SWANSEA & MUMBLES RAILWAY

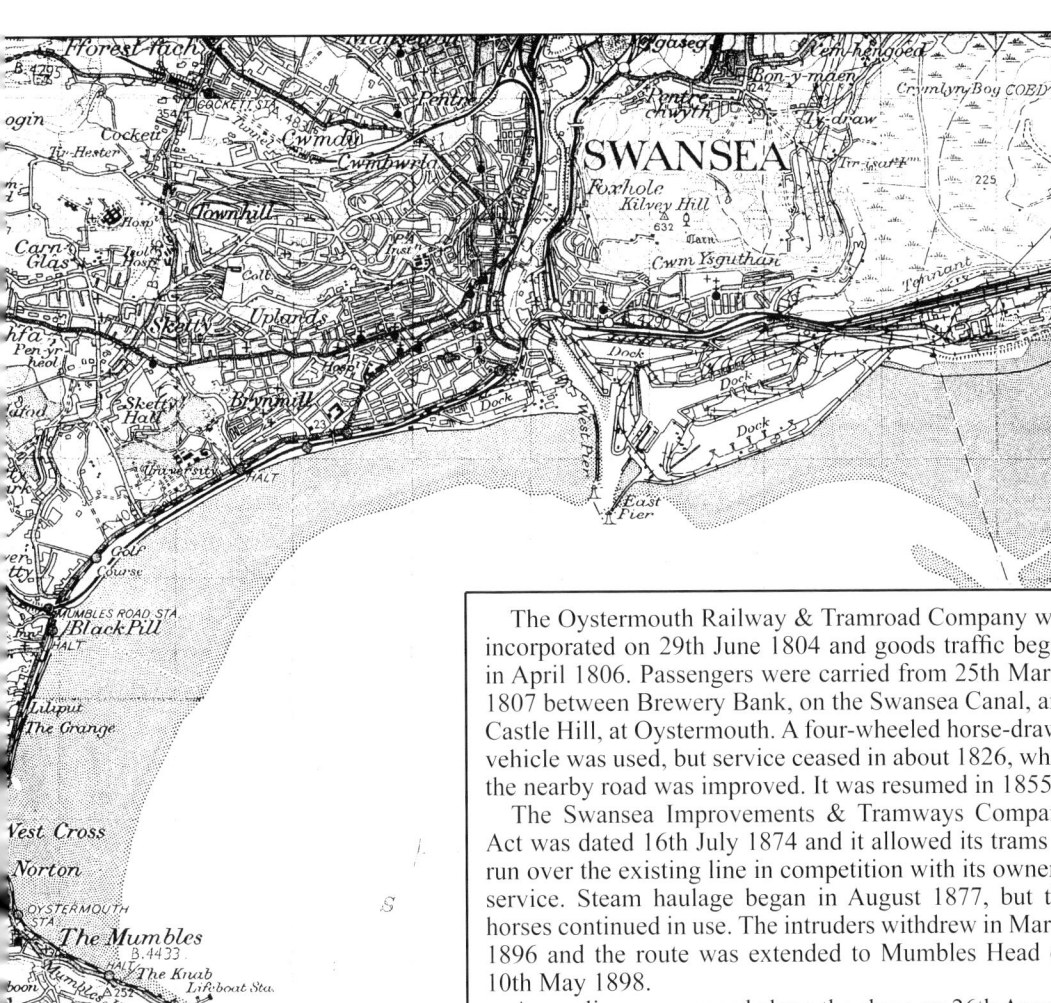

8a. The 1946 edition at 1ins to 1 mile names some of the stations, but shows others as halts and some are nameless. The university is close to the coast.

The Oystermouth Railway & Tramroad Company was incorporated on 29th June 1804 and goods traffic began in April 1806. Passengers were carried from 25th March 1807 between Brewery Bank, on the Swansea Canal, and Castle Hill, at Oystermouth. A four-wheeled horse-drawn vehicle was used, but service ceased in about 1826, when the nearby road was improved. It was resumed in 1855.

The Swansea Improvements & Tramways Company Act was dated 16th July 1874 and it allowed its trams to run over the existing line in competition with its owner's service. Steam haulage began in August 1877, but the horses continued in use. The intruders withdrew in March 1896 and the route was extended to Mumbles Head on 10th May 1898.

A new line was opened along the shore on 26th August 1900 and electric traction began on 2nd March 1929. Closure came on 5th January 1960, although Southend was the southern limit from 11th October 1959. Our journey is southwards, but devoid of station headings as most felt that they were on a tram trip. (I did in 1959!)

Passenger Services: This is illustrated by timetable extracts from Bradshaw.

The stations on the LMSR branch can be seen in the *Llandeilo to Swansea* album from Middleton Press.

8.1   We start with a glimpse at rolling stock evolution. The first car had been sketched as similar to a stage coach. It was notable as part of the first passenger railway in the world. This car is a development from that one and offered two classes, in the mid-1860s. (A.Dudman coll.)

8.2   The line was in the control of the Oystermouth Railway from 1st July 1877, but this was only for two years. The first Hughes tramway locomotive (right) was called *Pioneer* and was used on trial from 16th August 1877. Smoke and steam could not be issued on the journey and so a condenser was employed and coke firing was undertaken prior to a journey. (A.Dudman coll.)

8.3   An 0-4-0ST was built by Brush Electrical Engineering in 1907 and numbered 3. It is seen around 1910. In 1925, steam hauled 682,108 passengers, 8462 tons to coal and 532 tons of other goods. By 1938, the figures were 1,192,922, 492 and 38. With petrol rationing in 1945, passenger numbers rose to 4,237,000. (A.Dudman coll.)

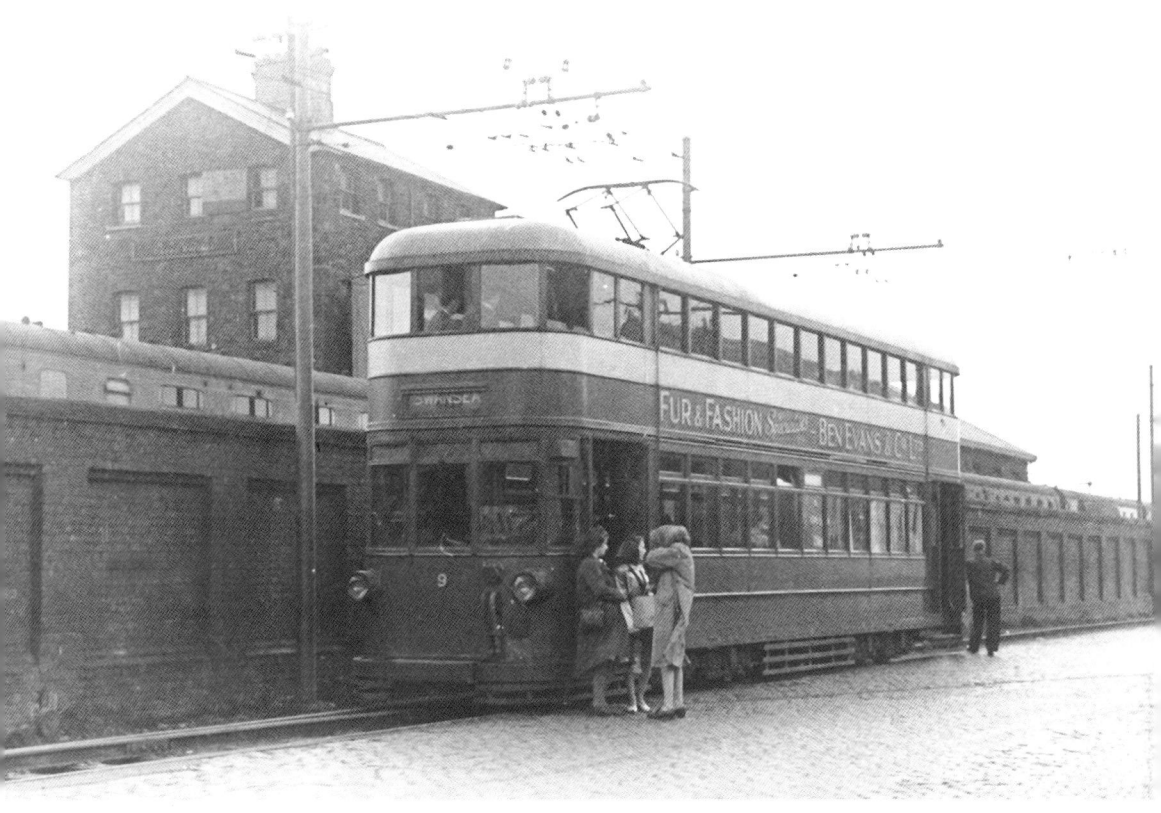

8.4   Our journey begins with five photographs at the **Rutland Street** terminus. This one has the former LNWR goods offices in the background. The goods shed of Victoria station had been leased to a banana importer in 1935. A train is berthed on a goods siding in 1947, when the street still had granite setts. (H.C.Casserley)

8.5   There were eleven cars initially and two more were added in 1930. They often ran in pairs, as seen. Unlike trams and most trains, all the doors were on one side. (T.J.Edgington)

8.6 Car 1 is nearest as we look at the connection to the depot on 28th August 1959. It also appears in four other photographs. The offices on the right also contained the waiting room. (S.P.Derek)

8.7 All passengers here had to board and alight in the road; one chose to walk in the middle of it! How times have changed. The freight connection to North Dock and East Dock continued beside the cars. (T.J.Edgington)

8.8 A Ford Consul passes close to the crowd boarding on 12th December 1959. The pipes on the front were for air brakes. The cars were built by Brush Electrical Engineering in Loughborough. (H.Ballantyne)

8.9 Left to right on the same day are nos 3, 11 and 12. Electrification was undertaken at 650 volts DC, but the new cars no longer offered a choice of classes. Battery electric propulsion had been tried in 1902.
(H.Ballantyne)

8.10 No. 1 is leaving Swansea on 12th July 1959 and is passing the photographer's 1934 Hillman 10. The former LNWR track is on the bank and signals are visible. The first two miles of the route to Sketty Road were single.
(H.C.Casserley)

8.11 No. 1 has called at **St. Helens** on 10th May 1951, before passsing under the bowstring footbridge in the background. Three ex-LNWR signals are included. The track was mostly single.
(H.C.Casserley)

8.12   A panorama from the bridge in the previous picture includes the platforms and crossover of the main line on 28th August 1959. This station was called "Swansea Bay", whereas the adjacent stop for S&MR services was **St. Gabriels**. This closed in 1912. (S.P.Derek)

Offices.—Rutland Street, Swansea.]   **SWANSEA and MUMBLES.**   [Sec., H. J. Westrup.
Swansea (Victoria Road and Rutland Street) to **Mumbles** at 5¾, 8 20, 9¾, and 11¼ mrn.; 1, 2 35, 3¼, 4½a, 5 35a, 6½a, 7 20a, and 9 aft.   SUNDAYS at 9 25 mrn.; 1, 3, 5 50, and 8¼ aft.
Mumbles to **Swansea** at 7, 9, and 10 20 mrn.; 12 10, 2, 3 10, 4½a, 5 35a, 6½a, 7 20a, 8 10, and 10 aft.   SUNDAYS at 10¼ mrn.; 2, 5, 7, and 9 30 aft.
FARES.—1st class, 8d.; 2nd class, 5d.   RETURN, 1s.; 8d.   *a* Stop at Passing Place.
☞ All 1&2 class, calling at Argyle Street, St. Helen's Road, Gorse Lane, Bryn Mill Road, Sketty Road, Mumbles Road, Black Pill, Lilliput Road, West Cross Road, Harold's Moor, and Norton Road.   Time of transit about 30 minutes.

August 1881

8b   The double track of the LNWR runs across this 1899 extract at 25ins to 1 mile and passes over the S&MR. The latter's goods yard has two sidings, which had a connection to the main line until 6th July 1952. W.M. indicates Weighing Machine. The track above Brook Villas ran to quarries in the Glyne Valley, where coal and limestone was produced.

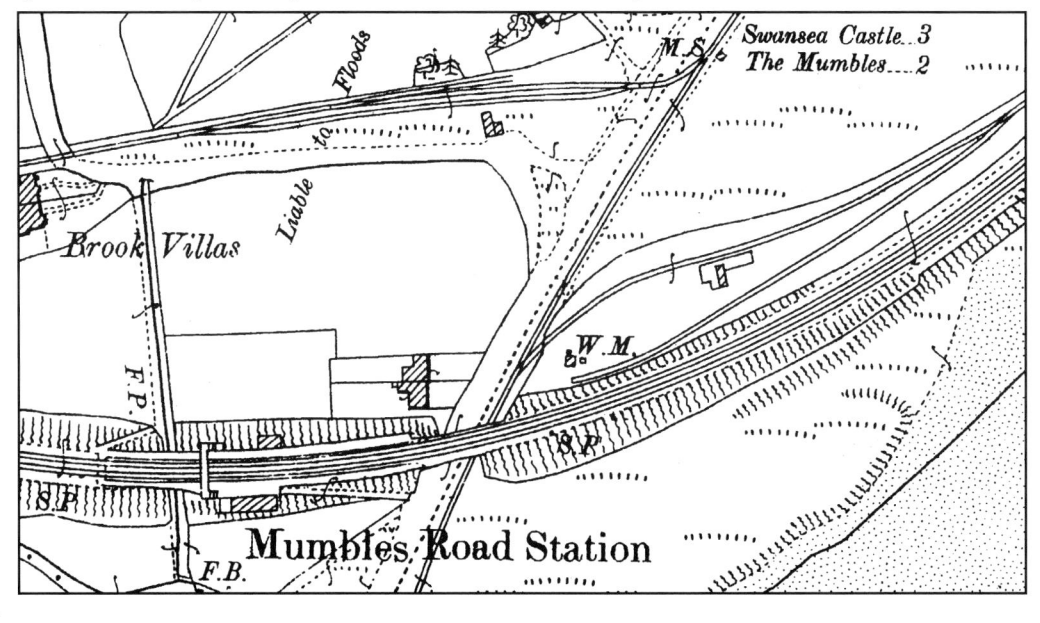

8.13   The bridge in the background carries the main line and is seen on the map. Cars 12 and 9 have passed under it on 26th August 1959 and will soon stop at Blackpill. This was the location of the rotary converter, which produced DC from AC for the power lines overhead. Admirers abound, including one beside the driver. (S.P.Derek)

8.14   No. 2 calls at **Blackpill** minutes later, the name being well above passenger eye level. This is our first view of the side devoid of doors. Steam ended in 1929 and the limited freight traffic was moved by a Hardy petrol 0-4-0 and from 1936 by a Fowler diesel 0-4-0 locomotive. (S.P.Derek)

8.15   Steam trains were up to 18 coaches long and could carry about 1200 passengers. By 1883, there were three locomotives, 67 horses and 25 cars. Seen at **Oystermouth** is one of the two 0-6-0Ts from the Hunslet Engine Company, which came in 1899 and were numbered 4 and 5. The first locomotives on the line were two 0-4-0STs from Hawthorn, Leslie, in 1892 and numbered 1 and 2. (P.Laming coll.)

December 1902

SWANSEA and MUMBLES.

Manager, David James.   Sec., J. W. Alison.

Swansea (Rutland Street) to **Mumbles** (Pier) at 8 20, 9 50, 10 30 (Saturdays only) and 11 25 mrn.; 12 10, 1 5, 2 15, 3 10, 4 10, 5 10, 6, 6 55, 7 45, 9 10, and 11 aft. SUNDAYS at 9 30 and 10 55 mrn.; 1, 2 5, 3 5, 4 5, 5 5, 5 50, 7 5, 8 10, and 9 5 aft.
Mumbles (Pier) to **Swansea** at 9 5, 10 25, and 11 20 (Saturdays only) mrn.; 12 5, 1, 2 10, 3 5, 4 5, 5 5, 5 55, 6 50, 7 40, 9 5, 10, and 11 40 aft. SUNDAYS at 10 15 mrn.; 12 10, 2, 3, 4, 5, 5 45, 7, 8 5, 9, and 10 aft.
☞ Trains call at Argyle Street, St. Helen's Road, St. Gabriels, Brynmill, Sketty Road, Mumbles Road (except Sundays), Blackpill, Lilliput, West Cross, Norton Road, Oystermouth, and Southend.

8.16   Car 10 was recorded loading at Oystermouth on 12th December 1959. The toilet facilities are surmounted by a substantial ventilator. Each car weighed 30 tons and had two motors. (H.Ballantyne)

8.17   Oystermouth is in the background as no. 10 runs towards the end of its journey at Southend on the same day, although the indicator suggests Mumbles Pier. The points and signalling system was automatic. The track from Mumbles Road to Mumbles Pier was mostly double, except at Norton Road. Cars swapped sides here. (H.Ballantyne)

8.18   Each car seated 106, 48 in the lower saloon and 58 on the top deck. Car 4 is receiving a group in raincoats in the final days of **Southend**. Southbound passengers would stand between the tracks. The stop is shown on map 8a as a halt, near The Knab. (T.J.Edgington)

8.19   We are on the bridge seen in picture 8.18 and witness the reversal of car 6 on 12th December 1959, while an AEC provides the competition. The cliff-foot route starts in the background. In the foreground is one of the signal huts and evidence of the fishing community. There were automatic facing point locks and extra rails to improve return current capacity. (H.Ballantyne)

August 1916

> **SWANSEA and MUMBLES.**
> Gen. Man., David James, Swansea.
> **Swansea** (Rutland St.) to Mumbles Pier at 4c30, 5c55, c7, 7c25, 8 15, 9 10, 10 10, and 11 10 mrn.: 12 10, 1 5, 2 5, 3, 3 45, 4 30, 5 15, 6 5, 7, 7 45, 8 30, 9 15, 9 10, and 11 b 5 aft.   SUNDAYS at 9 30 and 11 mrn.: 12 10, 1, 2 5, 2 40, 3 15, 4 5, 5 5, 5 50, 6 40, 7 30, 8 15, and 9 b 10 aft.   **Mumbles Pier to Swansea** (Rutland St.) at 5c15, 6c25, 7ac30, 8c10, 9 10, 10 10, and 11 10 mrn.; 12 10, 1, 2 5, 3, 3 45, 4 30, 5 15, 6 5, 7, 7 45, 8 30, 9 15, 10, 10b30, and 11b40 aft.   SUNDAYS at 10 15 mrn.: 12 10, 1, 2 5, 2 40, 3 15, 4 5, 5 5, 5 50, 6 40, 7 30, 8 15, 9 10, and 10b10 aft.
> *a* Calls at Mumbles Rd.   *b* To and from Southend.   *c* To and from Southend; stop at intermediate stations when required.
> ☞ Trains call at St. Helen's, St. Gabriel's, Brynmill, Blackpill, West Cross, Oystermouth (Station for Langland Bay and Caswell Bay), and Southend.

8.20   The pier opened with the extension of the S&MR to Mumbles Head. The terminus was called **Mumbles Pier** and its building is nearest on the right. The card had a postmark of 1909. (Stations UK)

8.21 Where better to enjoy the sound and aroma of a steam locomotive? We need say no more, apart from "Tickets please", perhaps. There were 39 such double deck cars at their optimum. (P.Laming coll.)

June 1920

SWANSEA and MUMBLES.
Gen. Man., David James, Swansea.

Swansea (Rutland St.) to Mumbles Pier at 4b30, 5b55, b7, 7$25, 8b15, 9 50, and 11 20 mrn.; 12 15, 1 5, 2 10, 3 10, 4 10, 5 10, 6 5, 6 55, 8 30, 9b40, and 10b45 aft. SUNDAYS at 9 30 and 11 mrn.; 1, 2 5, 3 5, 4 5, 5 5, 5 50, 6 40, 7 30, 8 15, and 9b10 aft.

Mumbles Pier to Swansea (Rutland St.) at 5b15, 6b25, 7b30, 8b10 (leaves Oystermouth at 8 23 mrn.), 9b5 (leaves Oystermouth at 9 15 mrn.), and 10 30 mrn.; 12 10, 1, 2 5, 3 5, 4 5, 5 5, 6, 6 50, 7 40, 9 5, 10b15, and 11b20 aft. SUNDAYS at 10 15 mrn.; 12 10, 2 5, 3, 4, 5, 5 45, 6 35, 7 25, 8 10, 9 5, and 9b50 aft.

b To and from Southend.

☞ Trains call at St. Helens, Brynmill, Blackpill, West Cross, Oystermouth (Station for Langland Bay and Caswell Bay), and Southend.

May 1944

SWANSEA and MUMBLES.—Mumbles Electric

Swansea (Rutland St.) to Mumbles Pier. WEEK DAYS at 4 40, 5 24, 5 47, 6 8, 6 31, 6 55, 7 27, 7 43, 7 51, 8 7, 8 15, 8 31, 8 55, 9 19, 9 43, 10 7, 10S23, 10E31, 10S39, 10 55, 11S11, 11E19, 11S27, 11 43, and 11S59 mrn; 12E7, 12S15, 12E23, 12S31, 12E39, 12S47, 12E55, 1 3, 1E11, 1S19, 1E27, 1S35, 1E43, 1 51, 2 7, 2 23, 2 39, 2 55, 3 11, 3 27, 3 43, 3 59, 4 15, 4 31, 4 47, 5 3, 5 19, 5 35, 5 51, 6 7, 6 23, 6 39, 6 55, 7 11, 7 27, 7 43, 7 59, 8 15, 8 31, 8 47, 9 3, 9 19, 9 35, 9 51, 10 7, 10 23, and 10 39 aft. SUNDAYS at 4 40, 5 47, 6 55, 9 19, 10 7, 10 31, 10 55, 11 19, and 11 43 mrn ; 12 7, 12 31, 12 55, 1 19, 1 43, 2 7, 2 23, 2 39, 2 55, 3 11, 3 27, 3 43, 3 59, 4 15, 4 31, 4 47, 5 3, 5 19, 5 35, 5 51, 6 7, 6 23, 6 39, 6 55, 7 11, 7 27, 7 43, 7 59, 8 15, 8 31, 8 47, 9 3, 9 19, 9 35, 9 51, 10 7, and 10 23 aft.

Mumbles Pier to Swansea (Rutland St.). WEEK DAYS at 52, 5 46, 6 7, 6 30, 6 54, 7 18, 7 50, 8 6, 8 14, 8 30, 8 38, 8 54, 9 18, 9 42, 10 6, 10 30, 10S46, 10E54, 11S2, 11 18, 11S34, 11E42, and 11S50 mrn ; 12 6, 12S22, 12E30, 12S38, 12E46, 12S54, 1E2, 1S10, 1E18, 1 26, 1 42, 1 55, 2E6, 2 14, 2 30, 2 46, 3 2, 3 18, 3 34, 3 60, 4 6, 4 22, 4 38, 4 54, 5 10, 5 26, 5 42, 5 58, 6 14, 6 30, 6 46, 7 2, 7 18, 7 34, 7 50, 8 6, 8 22, 8 38, 8 54, 9 10, 9 26, 9 42, 9 58, 10 14, 10 30, 10 46, and 11 2 aft. SUNDAYS at 5 2, 6 14, 7 18, 9 42, 10 30, 10 54, 11 18, and 11 42 mrn ; 12 6, 12 30, 12 54, 1 18, 1 42, 2 6, 2 30, 2 46, 3 2, 3 18, 3 34, 3 50, 4 6, 4 22, 4 38, 4 50, 5 10, 5 26, 5 42, 5 58, 6 14, 6 34, 6 46, 7 2, 7 18, 7 34, 7 50, 8 2, 8 22, 8 38, 8 54, 9 10, 9 26, 9 46, 9 58, 10 14, 10 30, and 10 46 aft. E Except Saturdays. S Saturdays only.

☞ Trains call at St. Helens 4, Brynmill 6, Ashleigh Rd. 9, Blackpill 11, West Cross 13, Norton Rd. 14, Oystermouth (Sta. for Langland Bay and Caswell Bay) 16, Southend 17 and arr Mumbles Pier 19 mins. after leaving Swansea (R. St.).

8.22 The 835ft long pier was renovated in 1987-88, but there is little trace of the terminus now. Sadly the crowds have gone for ever. Almost 14,000 signatures were obtained on a petition against closure, but it went ahead, despite two successful railway revivals in North Wales showing the potential. (Stations UK)

MP Middleton Press
EVOLVING THE ULTIMATE RAIL ENCYCLOPEDIA

Easebourne Lane, Midhurst, West Sussex.
GU29 9AZ   Tel:01730 813169
www.middletonpress.co.uk   email:info@middletonpress.co.uk
A-978 0 906520 B- 978 1 873793 C- 978 1 901706 D-978 1 904474
E - 978 1 906008   F - 978 1 908174

All titles listed below were in print at time of publication - please check current availability by looking at our website - www.middletonpress.co.uk or by requesting a Brochure which includes our LATEST RAILWAY TITLES also our TRAMWAY, TROLLEYBUS, MILITARY and COASTAL series

A
Abergavenny to Merthyr C 91 8
Abertillery & Ebbw Vale Lines D 84 5
Aberystwyth to Carmarthen E 90 1
Allhallows - Branch Line to A 62 8
Alton - Branch Lines to A 11 6
Andover to Southampton A 82 6
Ascot - Branch Lines around A 64 2
Ashburton - Branch Line to B 95 4
Ashford - Steam to Eurostar B 67 1
Ashford to Dover A 48 2
Austrian Narrow Gauge D 04 3
Avonmouth - BL around D 42 5
Aylesbury to Rugby D 91 3

B
Baker Street to Uxbridge D 90 6
Bala to Llandudno E 87 1
Banbury to Birmingham D 27 2
Banbury to Cheltenham E 63 5
Bangor to Holyhead F 01 7
Bangor to Portmadoc E 72 7
Barking to Southend C 80 2
Barmouth to Pwllheli E 53 6
Barry - Branch Lines around D 50 0
Bartlow - Branch Lines to F 27 7
Bath Green Park to Bristol C 36 9
Bath to Evercreech Junction A 60 4
Beamish 40 years on rails E94 9
Bedford to Wellingborough D 31 9
Birmingham to Wolverhampton E253
Bletchley to Cambridge D 94 4
Bletchley to Rugby E 07 9
Bodmin - Branch Lines around B 83 1
Bournemouth to Evercreech Jn A 46 8
Bournemouth to Weymouth A 57 4
Bradshaw's Guide 1866 F 05 5
Bradshaw's History F18 5
Bradshaw's Rail Times 1850 F 13 0
Bradshaw's Rail Times 1895 F 11 6
Branch Lines series - see town names
Brecon to Neath D 43 2
Brecon to Newport D 16 6
Brecon to Newtown E 06 2
Brighton to Eastbourne A 16 1
Brighton to Worthing A 03 1
Bristol to Taunton D 03 6
Bromley South to Rochester B 23 7
Bromsgrove to Birmingham D 87 6
Bromsgrove to Gloucester D 73 9
Broxbourne to Cambridge F16 1
Brunel - A railtour D 74 6
Bude - Branch Line to B 29 9
Burnham to Evercreech Jn B 68 0

C
Cambridge to Ely D 55 5
Canterbury - BLs around B 58 9
Cardiff to Dowlais (Cae Harris) E 47 5
Cardiff to Pontypridd E 95 6
Cardiff to Swansea E 42 0
Carlisle to Hawick E 85 7
Carmarthen to Fishguard E 66 6
Caterham & Tattenham Corner B251
Central & Southern Spain NG E 91 8
Chard and Yeovil - BLs a C 30 7
Charing Cross to Dartford A 75 8
Charing Cross to Orpington A 96 3
Cheddar - Branch Line to B 90 9
Cheltenham to Andover C 43 7
Cheltenham to Redditch D 81 4
Chester to Birkenhead F 21 5
Chester to Rhyl E 93 2
Chichester to Portsmouth A 14 7
Clacton and Walton - BLs to F 04 8
Clapham Jn to Beckenham Jn B 36 7
Cleobury Mortimer - BLs a E 18 5
Clevedon & Portishead - BLs to D180
Consett to South Shields E 57 4
Cornwall Narrow Gauge D 56 2
Corris and Vale of Rheidol E 65 9
Craven Arms to Llandeilo E 35 2
Craven Arms to Wellington E 33 8
Crawley to Littlehampton A 34 5
Cromer - Branch Lines around C 26 0
Croydon to East Grinstead B 48 0
Crystal Palace & Catford Loop B 87 1
Cyprus Narrow Gauge E 13 0

D
Darjeeling Revisited F 09 3
Darlington Leamside Newcastle E 28 4
Darlington to Newcastle D 98 2
Dartford to Sittingbourne B 34 3
Denbigh - Branch Lines around F 32 1
Derwent Valley - BL to the D 06 7
Devon Narrow Gauge E 09 3
Didcot to Banbury D 02 9
Didcot to Swindon C 84 0
Didcot to Winchester C 13 0
Dorset & Somerset NG D 76 0
Douglas - Laxey - Ramsey E 75 8
Douglas to Peel C 88 8
Douglas to Port Erin C 55 0
Douglas to Ramsey D 39 5
Dover to Ramsgate A 78 9
Dublin Northwards in 1950s E 31 4
Dunstable - Branch Lines E 27 7

E
Ealing to Slough C 42 0
Eastbourne to Hastings A 27 7
East Cornwall Mineral Railways D 22 7
East Croydon to Three Bridges A 53 6
Eastern Spain Narrow Gauge E 56 7
East Grinstead - BLs to A 07 9
East London - Branch Lines of C 44 4
East London Line B 80 0
East of Norwich - Branch Lines E 69 7
Effingham Junction - BLs a A 74 1
Ely to Norwich C 90 1
Enfield Town & Palace Gates D 32 6
Epsom to Horsham A 30 7
Eritrean Narrow Gauge E 38 3
Euston to Harrow & Wealdstone C 89 5
Exeter to Barnstaple B 15 2
Exeter to Newton Abbot C 49 9
Exeter to Tavistock B 69 5
Exmouth - Branch Lines to B 00 8

F
Fairford - Branch Line to A 52 9
Falmouth, Helston & St. Ives C 74 1
Fareham to Salisbury A 67 3
Faversham to Dover B 05 3
Felixstowe & Aldeburgh - BL to D 20 3
Fenchurch Street to Barking C 20 8
Festiniog - 50 yrs of enterprise C 83 3
Festiniog 1946-55 E 01 7
Festiniog in the Fifties B 68 8
Festiniog in the Sixties B 91 6
Ffestiniog in Colour 1955-82 F 25 3
Finsbury Park to Alexandra Pal C 02 8
Frome to Bristol B 77 0

G
Gloucester to Bristol D 35 7
Gloucester to Cardiff D 66 1
Gosport - Branch Lines around A 36 9
Greece Narrow Gauge D 72 2

H
Hampshire Narrow Gauge D 36 4
Harrow to Watford D 14 2
Harwich & Hadleigh - BLs to F 02 4
Hastings to Ashford A 37 6
Hawick to Galashiels F 36 9
Hawkhurst - Branch Line to A 66 6
Hayling - Branch Line to A 12 3
Hay-on-Wye - BL around D 92 0
Haywards Heath to Seaford A 28 4
Hemel Hempstead - BLs to D 88 3
Henley, Windsor & Marlow - BLa C77 2
Hereford to Newport D 54 8
Hertford & Hatfield - BLs a E 58 1
Hertford Loop E 71 0
Hexham to Carlisle D 75 3
Hexham to Hawick F 08 6
Hitchin to Peterborough D 07 4
Holborn Viaduct to Lewisham A 81 9
Horsham - Branch Lines to A 02 4
Huntingdon - Branch Line to A 93 2

I
Ilford to Shenfield C 97 0
Ilfracombe - Branch Line to B 21 3
Industrial Rlys of the South East A 09 3
Ipswich to Saxmundham C 41 3
Isle of Wight Lines - 50 yrs C 12 3
Italy Narrow Gauge F 17 8

K
Kent Narrow Gauge C 45 1
Kidderminster to Shrewsbury E 10 9
Kingsbridge - Branch Line to C 98 7
Kings Cross to Potters Bar E 62 8
Kingston & Hounslow Loops A 83 3
Kingswear - Branch Line to C 17 8

L
Lambourn - Branch Line to C 70 3
Launceston & Princetown - BLs C 19 2
Lewisham to Dartford A 92 5
Lines around Wimbledon B 75 6
Liverpool Street to Chingford D 01 2
Liverpool Street to Ilford C 34 5
Llandeilo to Swansea E 46 8
London Bridge to Addiscombe B 20 6
London Bridge to East Croydon A 58 1
Longmoor - Branch Lines to A 41 3
Looe - Branch Line to C 22 2
Lowestoft - BLs around E 40 6
Ludlow to Hereford E 14 7
Lydney - Branch Lines around E 26 0
Lyme Regis - Branch Line to A 45 1
Lynton - Branch Line to B 04 6

M
Machynlleth to Barmouth E 54 3
Maesteg and Tondu Lines E 06 2
March - Branch Lines around B 09 1
Marylebone to Rickmansworth D 49 4
Melton Constable to Yarmouth Bch E031
Midhurst - Branch Lines of E 78 9
Midhurst - Branch Lines to F 00 0
Mitcham Junction Lines B 01 5
Mitchell & company C 59 8
Monmouth - Branch Lines to E 20 8
Monmouthshire Eastern Valleys D 71 5
Moretonhampstead - BL to C 27 7
Moreton-in-Marsh to Worcester D 26 5
Mountain Ash to Neath D 80 7

N
Newbury to Westbury C 66 6
Newcastle to Hexham D 69 2
Newport (IOW) - Branch Lines to A 26 0
Newquay - Branch Lines to C 71 0
Newton Abbot to Plymouth C 60 4
Newtown to Aberystwyth E 41 3
North East German NG D 44 9
Northern Alpine Narrow Gauge F 37 6
Northern France Narrow Gauge C 75 8
Northern Spain Narrow Gauge E 83 3
North London Line B 94 7
North Woolwich - BLs around C 65 9

O
Ongar - Branch Line to E 05 5
Oswestry - Branch Lines around E 60 4
Oswestry to Whitchurch E 81 9
Oxford to Bletchley D 57 9
Oxford to Moreton-in-Marsh D 15 9

P
Paddington to Ealing C 37 6
Paddington to Princes Risborough C819
Padstow - Branch Line to B 54 1
Pembroke and Cardigan - BLs to F 29 1
Peterborough to Kings Lynn E 32 1
Plymouth - BLs around B 98 5
Plymouth to St. Austell C 63 5
Pontypool to Mountain Ash D 65 4
Pontypridd to Merthyr F 14 7
Pontypridd to Port Talbot E 84 6
Porthmadog 1954-94 - BLa B 31 2
Portmadoc 1923-46 - BLa B 13 8
Portsmouth to Southampton A 31 4
Portugal Narrow Gauge E 67 3
Potters Bar to Cambridge D 70 8
Princes Risborough - BL to D 05 0
Princes Risborough to Banbury C 85 7

R
Reading to Basingstoke B 27 5
Reading to Didcot C 79 6
Reading to Guildford A 47 5
Redhill to Ashford A 73 4
Return to Blaenau 1970-82 C 64 2
Rhyl to Bangor F 15 4
Rhymney & New Tredegar Lines E 48 2
Rickmansworth to Aylesbury D 61 6
Romania & Bulgaria NG E 23 9
Romneyrail C 32 1
Ross-on-Wye - BLs around E 30 7
Ruabon to Barmouth E 84 0
Rugby to Birmingham E 37 6
Rugby to Loughborough F 12 3
Rugby to Stafford F 07 9
Ryde to Ventnor A 19 2

S
Salisbury to Westbury B 39 8
Saxmundham to Yarmouth C 69 7
Saxony Narrow Gauge D 47 0
Seaton & Sidmouth - BLs to A 95 6
Selsey - Branch Line to A 04 8
Sheerness - Branch Line to B 16 2
Shenfield to Ipswich E 96 3
Shrewsbury - Branch Line to A 86 4
Shrewsbury to Chester E 70 3
Shrewsbury to Ludlow E 21 5
Shrewsbury to Newtown E 29 1
Sierra Leone Narrow Gauge D 28 9
Sirhowy Valley Line E 12 3
Sittingbourne to Ramsgate A 90 1
Slough to Newbury C 56 7
South African Two-foot gauge E 51 2
Southampton to Bournemouth A 42 0
Southend & Southminster BLs E 76 5
Southern Alpine Narrow Gauge F 22 2
Southern France Narrow Gauge C 47 5
South London Line B 46 6
South Lynn to Norwich City F 03 1

Southwold - Branch Line to A 1
Spalding - Branch Lines around
Stafford to Chester F 34 5
St Albans to Bedford D 08 1
St. Austell to Penzance C 67 3
ST Isle of Wight A 56 7
Stourbridge to Wolverhampton
St. Pancras to Barking D 68 5
St. Pancras to Folkestone E 88
St. Pancras to St. Albans C 78
Stratford-u-Avon to Birmingham
Stratford-u-Avon to Cheltenham
ST West Hants A 69 7
Sudbury - Branch Lines to F 19
Surrey Narrow Gauge C 87 1
Sussex Narrow Gauge C 68 0
Swanley to Ashford B 45 9
Swansea to Carmarthen E 59 8
Swindon to Bristol C 96 3
Swindon to Gloucester D 46 3
Swindon to Newport D 30 2
Swiss Narrow Gauge C 94 9

T
Talyllyn 60 E 98 7
Taunton to Barnstaple B 60 2
Taunton to Exeter C 82 6
Tavistock to Plymouth B 88 6
Tenterden - Branch Line to A 21
Three Bridges to Brighton A 35
Tilbury Loop C 86 4
Tiverton - BLs around C 62 8
Tivetshall to Beccles D 41 8
Tonbridge to Hastings A 44 4
Torrington - Branch Lines to B 3
Towcester - BLs around E 39 0
Tunbridge Wells BLs A 32 1

U
Upwell - Branch Line to B 64 0

V
Victoria to Bromley South A 98
Vivarais Revisited E 08 6

W
Wantage - Branch Line to D 25
Wareham to Swanage 50 yrs D
Waterloo to Windsor A 54 3
Waterloo to Woking A 38 3
Watford to Leighton Buzzard D
Welshpool to Llanfair E 49 9
Wenford Bridge to Fowey C 09
Westbury to Bath B 55 8
Westbury to Taunton C 76 5
West Cornwall Mineral Rlys D 4
West Croydon to Epsom B 08 4
West German Narrow Gauge D
West London - BLs of C 50 5
West London Line B 84 8
West London Line B 848
West Wiltshire - BLs of D 12 8
Weymouth - BLs A 65 9
Willesden Jn to Richmond B 71
Wimbledon to Beckenham C 58
Wimbledon to Epsom B 62 6
Wimborne - BLs around A 97 0
Wisbech - BLs around C 01 7
Witham & Kelvedon - BLs a E 4
Woking to Alton A 59 8
Woking to Portsmouth A 25 3
Woking to Southampton A 55 0
Wolverhampton to Shrewsbury
Worcester to Birmingham D 97
Worcester to Hereford D 38 8
Worthing to Chichester A 06 2
Wroxham - BLs around F 31 4

Y
Yeovil - 50 yrs change C 38 3
Yeovil to Dorchester B 76 5
Yeovil to Exeter A 91 8
York to Scarborough F 23 9

96